THE FIVE SECRETS
TO FINDING A JOB

THE FIVE SECRETS TO FINDING A JOB
A Story of Success

Barbara L. Siegel

with

Robert S. Siegel

IMPACT PUBLICATIONS
Manassas Park, VA

THE FIVE SECRETS TO FINDING A JOB:
A Story of Success

All rights reserved. Printed in the United States of America. No part of this book may be used or reproduced in any manner whatsoever without written permission of the publisher: IMPACT PUBLICATIONS, 9104-N Manassas Drive, Manassas Park, VA 22111, Tel. 703/361-7300.

Library of Congress Cataloguing-in-Publication Data

Siegel, Barbara L.
  The five secrets to finding a job: a story of success/Barbara L. Siegel with Robert S. Siegel.
       p.   cm.
  Includes index.
  ISBN 0-942710-96-7 : $12.95
  1. Applications for positions. 2. Résumés (Employment). 3. Employment interviewing. 4. Job hunting. I. Siegel, Robert S. II. Title. III. Title: 5 secrets to finding a job.
  HF5382.7.S55   1994
  650.14—dc20   93-29359
                                                              CIP

For information on distribution or quantity discount rates, Tel. 703/361-7300, Fax 703/335-9486, or write to: Sales Department, IMPACT PUBLICATIONS, 9104-N Manassas Drive, Manassas Park, VA 22111. Distributed to the trade by National Book Network, 4720 Boston Way, Suite A, Lanham, MD 20706, Tel. 301/459-8696.

CONTENTS

EXHIBITS

ACKNOWLEDGEMENT

I wish to thank my dear friend, Mary Jo Colagiovanni, for the many hours she spent reading this manuscript and advising me on ways to make the writing more clear and concise. Mary Jo not only brought a highly objective and wonderfully analytical eye to the work, but she also communicated her observations in a positive and motivating way, refreshing my energy and excitement as I continued to write.

Mary Jo's contribution to this book was invaluable, and I will always remain deeply appreciative of her friendship and of all I learned from her.

INTRODUCTION

Our goal in developing this material in an easy-to-read story form is to prepare you for the job market in a way that will be enjoyable yet effective. But please realize that just reading the information is not enough. To really benefit from this book, you will need to complete the exercises suggested at the end of each chapter and then go out into the job market and apply what you have learned. As you will see, the characters in the book complete all the exercises in one weekend. We do not expect you to do that.

Naturally, as each of you is different, so will be the pace at which you each will complete the exercises. Remember, it is more important that you do each exercise thoroughly than that you finish in a given amount of time.

Before you start reading, please put together a Job Success Notebook consisting of a three ring binder and paper. You may also want to get some dividers for later use. As you get into your job search, feel free to organize your notebook to suit your needs.

Bob and I hope that reading this book is the beginning of a positive adventure in your life.

Chapter One

UNEMPLOYED!

"Beth, today is your last day. I have to let you go. It's the decision of the home office. I'm sorry, but I think it will be best for everyone."

I looked at John in disbelief. I came into his office this morning prepared to give him new ideas on reorganizing the filing system, and instead he was firing me? This couldn't be happening. I have made so many improvements in the year since I walked in the front door.

"Why?" I asked hoping to hear an answer like, "You are so bright and innovative, and such a good leader, that we don't deserve you." What I heard was, "The girls just don't like you."

The words slapped me in the face even though I knew what he said was true. I knew it the day I came for a second interview and they looked at me with suspicious eyes. I knew it the day I started and received a chilled welcome, and again when I came back from two weeks of training at the home office and faced stony resistance to the changes I was asked to implement. I knew it when I took them out to lunch at Christmas and the conversation was strained into a formal politeness. I always knew it, I just thought I could overcome it in time.

When I walked in the door of this small mortgage banking firm a year ago, stacks of work were piled everywhere. The branch was understaffed for the volume of loans it wrote and it was also in need of more space. John Rait was the Branch Manager: a nice looking gentleman in his early sixties trying desperately not to rock the boat before his retirement. I was hired as the Office Manager, a newly created position that had been first offered to 'the girls' but none of them wanted it. Unfortunately, they knew who their leader was, and it sure wasn't going to be me. I never did figure out why the young woman who was clearly the office leader had not officially taken the job. I was told she didn't want responsibility for managing people (perhaps because her sister was one of the 'people'), but it was apparent that she would not truly relinquish her position of authority with the other women. I had tried to move forward in spite of this. I managed to convince the home office that we needed more staff, got them to expand into some vacant space next door, and even won overtime payment so we could get the work caught up. I thought the women would come around, especially when they earned more money, but it didn't make any difference. In fact, it seemed to backfire. The more I did, the more resentment I felt. But to actually fire me, I couldn't believe it, and John, the whimp, wasn't going to stand up to anyone. I had made him look good, and now he was showing me the door! I felt the tears brimming up in my eyes. They were from anger as much as hurt, and I hated those tears because of the weakness he would interpret them to mean.

"Beth," he said, "take the rest of the day off and come back at 5:00 p.m. to clean out your desk. I don't want to make you do it in front of the girls."

I couldn't trust my voice to talk and so I looked at him with a look I hoped would penetrate him to his soul, a look he would have to carry with him for his entire life, a look of anger, hurt, and disgust. Then I got up and walked out of his office, went to my desk, got my purse, and went to my car.

As I drove to my apartment, thoughts of anger and revenge filled my mind. I discovered myself at my front door and found the appropriate key to let myself in. I was glad Andy was at school. I know if he had been home, I would have let all my feelings pour out onto him. For a ten year old boy that might be too much to handle, especially from one's mother. The cat looked at me with total indifference. I went into my bedroom, got the box of kleenex and the phone, plopped down in the middle of my bed and dialed Jessica.

As the phone rang, I thought about how Jessica had started at her computer software firm in much the same position as I had at my firm, but her ideas got her promotions. She eventually went into sales and now was not only her firm's top seller, but she was also sent around the country to their other branches to do sales training.

"Unified Data, may I help you?"

"Jessica Turney, please." I heard the traditional canned music as I was put on hold.

"Jessica Turney" came the familiar voice.

"Jessica, they fired me!"

"Beth, I'm sorry, really I am. What did they say?"

I told Jessica about the morning events, and how much I hated John for being so weak, and how mad I was at myself for not being able to talk up to him in his office because of stupid tears (which now were no longer there). I told her how I had to go back at 5:00 p.m. (which felt like both a blessing and a curse) and how worried I was about money, and how anxious I was about getting a new job.

Jessica was wonderful. She let me get it all out without interrupting me once. When I was done she said; "Beth, I will help you to get a job, but you must trust me. Okay?"

"Okay," I said, not seeing any better alternative anyway.

"Great! Then here is the plan. First of all, I want you to go out today. It's only 11:00 a.m. and you have a long way to go until 5:00 p.m. I already have a lunch appointment, and I have to give a training seminar this afternoon, so you are on your own. But, Beth, you need to be kind to yourself now. I want you to go someplace you enjoy for lunch and then treat yourself to a matinee. That should take up most of your afternoon. Don't sit in that apartment! At 5:00, collect your things and pick Andy up at his after-school program like you always do. I suggest you don't tell him what happened yet; let's you and I talk first. Why don't you call Rob and tell him that you need him to take Andy this weekend. Since it's Friday, Andy won't think anything of it. It's up to you whether you want to tell Rob what happened, although if you do tell him, he may be more accommodating about taking Andy on such short notice. I'll meet you for dinner at Reuben's at 7:00, and together we will spend the weekend working out a plan for your job hunt. Does this sound okay to you?"

"Except for the part where I have to tell Rob I failed at my job ('as well as our marriage,' I imagined Rob thinking) it sounds fine. Jessica, I really appreciate your support, I know you are very busy at work."

"Beth, you were there for me when I was down, and I am glad I have the opportunity to return the favor. I'll see you

* * *

"I hope you will see this

as an opportunity . . . "

* * *

later. And, Beth, I have to tell you I am glad that job is over. There was no place for you to go there, and I don't think you would have ever been happy. You were fighting a losing battle from day one. This may sound silly, but I hope you will see this as an opportunity to move into a position where you won't be so stifled and on the defensive all the time."

"Thanks, Jessica. I will try to think about it that way. You better get back to work or you will be looking for a job with me. See you later."

Before you continue . . .

Can you see an opportunity to improve yourself and/or your situation in this career move? If so, what is it? Take some time to think about this and write down your answer in your Job Success Notebook. Writing often helps focus your thoughts.

Also, plan to do something nice for yourself within the week.

Chapter Two

SELL YOURSELF— THE 5 SECRET STEPS TO FINDING A JOB

"Beth, Hi! How did it go?" Jessica asked as she sat down at the table I had gotten for us at Reuben's. "Did you stick to the plan?"

"Hi, Jessica. Yes, I did just what you said. I called Rob, and he was really very nice and understanding. After I made arrangements with Rob to take care of Andy, I felt more relaxed. I went to The China Garden for their lunch special, and then I went across to the mall to a matinee. When the movie was over, I went back to the office with the obligatory cardboard box. As usual for Friday, the office cleared out about 4:55 p.m. and only John was there. While I had been drinking my tea at China Garden, I had given a lot of thought to what I would say when John and I were alone, and I decided not to try to talk to him about the decision to let me go. We both knew what really happened in that office, and I knew he would have to be on the defensive, and I would just get angry all over again.

"John watched me the whole time I cleaned out my desk. That was humiliating. I did ask him if he thought it was necessary, after all, I didn't think the company had any secrets I would care to steal. He smiled and said he knew I could be trusted, but (as usual) he was just carrying out company policy. I don't think John ever had an idea that wasn't already company policy. I told him that. He just smiled. When I left, I was glad I had not gotten into a fighting match with him; the fact that I had some control over my emotions made me feel stronger.

"I picked up Andy and took him to Rob's. I told him I had to do some extra work over the weekend. I got here about 6:30, got our table and ordered a glass of wine. Since then, I have been sitting here sipping the wine and thinking about what has happened and what is going to happen. You know, I have to admit, there is a part of me that feels a great sense of relief. It's over. I don't know if I could have quit. After my marriage fell apart, I wanted to feel I could stick to something, even if I was unhappy with it."

"Beth, I know you feel you have to prove you are a capable person, but I don't agree that sticking to something at any cost proves anything. My hope is that you will realize that you are a bright, worthwhile, likable person, something that those of us who are your friends already know."

"Thanks. I appreciate hearing that because I don't think I am likable, at least not in the way that you are. Everyone seems to want to be around you. I've never had people come to me in the same way that they come to you."

"Maybe you won't ever have people fluttering around you, Beth. You are a much more private person than I am, but that doesn't mean they don't like you, and it certainly doesn't mean you can't be a good manager! When you look at what happened in this job, I hope you realize that those women would not have liked anyone. It would not have mattered if it was me or you, the person walking into that position was doomed. For whatever reason, they were angry and hostile before you arrived on the scene. They probably never even tried to assess you as a person because they were too busy being mad at the position."

"Do you really believe that?"

"Yes, I do. I have seen similar problems in some of our small branches. I'm really not sure why the dynamics of small groups often works against the establishment, but one thing I am sure about is that I have never met anyone who got fired that didn't have ego damage over it, and knowing you, you will definitely have some. But, I hope you limit it and try to let it go. For the next couple of weeks or even months, you will have to make a conscious effort not to get lost in negative thinking. When you find that you are putting

* * *

"... make a conscious
effort not to get lost
in negative thinking."

* * *

yourself down for what has happened, think about something else, anything else: what you are going to make for dinner, where you want to take Andy for fun, anything but what a 'failure' you are. Remember, Beth, people are fired everyday, people you look at and admire and probably even envy. If we went to a party of all our friends and everyone who ever got fired or laid off had to declare it under some truth serum, I think you would be shocked at the number. I bet it would be at least 50%."

"Really? You think so?"

"Definitely, I'd put money on it."

"Well, that certainly makes me feel better!"

"May I take your order, ladies?" the waiter asked.

"I'll have the Chinese Chicken Salad and iced tea," said Jessica.

"I think I have had my quota of Chinese for the day. I'll have the grilled chicken sandwich and coffee with regular milk instead of cream, please. Thanks."

"Jessica, what is it we are going to do all weekend to get me ready for this job hunt?"

"Well," Jessica looked a little sheepish. "Now don't get mad until you hear me out...I am going to give you a crash course in sales training."

"Jessica! You know how I feel about sales! I don't want to be a salesperson. As you pointed out, I'm too private a person."

"Just because you are private doesn't mean you can't be dynamic. Remember, don't keep putting yourself down. Try to stay open to new ideas. You might be surprised at the career fields you may really enjoy if you learned more about them. Personally, I think you would be a fabulous sales person. You are well organized, you have the ability to be empathic, and people trust you. But, I am not planning to train you to be a salesperson, instead, I am going to train you in sales skills, so that you can sell yourself into a job you would like."

Just then the waiter came with the food, which looked delicious. As soon as he put it down and left, I said: "What do you mean, 'sell myself into a job I would like'. What has sales got to do with getting a new job?"

"Beth, sales has everything to do with it. When you are out in the job market, you are selling your skills and abilities to solve the problems and meet the needs of the employer. The people who realize this and use it to their advantage are the ones who will get the best jobs. Most people go on a job interview wondering what the company will do for them: what benefits they will get, how much they will be paid, and what hours they will be expected to work. In other words, they are entirely focused on their own needs and desires and that's what comes across when they interview. Employers, however, are worried about their company's needs. They want to find a person who will put the company's needs first and then take responsibility for meeting those needs. The person who can go in for the interview and approach it from the employer's perspective is going to be way ahead of his or her competition.

"This is where I believe that job hunting skills and sales skills are the same. When I hear salespeople moaning about how they can't make sales, I am pretty sure that when they go into a sales situation all they are worried about is making the sale. What I tell them is to stop worrying about making the sale and start worrying about what the customer wants. I think the same holds true when I hear someone tell me they can't find a job; I am usually pretty sure he or she goes into an interview with a 'what are you going to do for me attitude.' Does this make sense to you?"

"Yes, it really does. I know when I interviewed individuals for the clerical position we had available, I was really turned off by the people who started asking me about salary and benefits before we had even discussed the responsibilities of the job. The person I ended up hiring was someone who came in with a lot of enthusiasm and was obviously anxious to please."

"Well, I am glad you see what I am talking about when I tell you that sales skills will transfer into job hunting skills. I think, when we get into it, you will find this not only interesting but really a lot of fun!"

"Jessica, what else do I have to know about sales?"

"First of all, let me give you a brief overview of how I see the sales process and how it relates to job hunting. Then we will go into it in-depth. I teach the sales process in five basic steps, and what I teach as the five basic sales steps, I think you will discover are the five secret steps to finding a job. The first step is knowing the product. You certainly can't sell something you have very little knowledge of. In the job market, you are the product, and you must be aware of your skills and abilities. That may sound simple, but most people really never take stock of their abilities. Once you know the product, then you need to develop sales tools to present the product to the buyer, such as your resume, a portfolio, or whatever is appropriate to your field. The third step involves developing a prospect list. Who would need what you have to offer? Part of the prospect list is also determining what kind of environment you would like to be in. Now, you are ready for the sales call. The sales call itself has two parts—first, you need to set the appointment with the prospect, and second, you give your presentation (in job hunting terms, giving the presentation is conducting the interview) at the appointed time. The fifth and final step of the sale is the close. This is where you ask for the sale, which in your case amounts to asking for the job, negotiate the price, meaning your salary, and, lastly, accept or reject the terms, or in job market language, accept or reject the employer's offer.

"Beth, I noticed that you brought in your notebook. I think it would be helpful if you wrote down a few notes so that you will have them to refer to. I am also going to give you a homework assignment for tonight."

"I knew this was going to get harder," I laughed as the waiter removed our plates.

"Can I get you ladies dessert?" he asked.

"Just a refill on my coffee and some more iced tea for my friend," I replied.

Jessica got very serious when she talked about sales. Anyone listening would know she had a passion for it. She was truly a 'professional' salesperson and I respected her for her knowledge and integrity.

"First off," Jessica said, "I think it would be good for you to write down the sales steps in brief, so you can refer to them often to keep yourself on track."

As she repeated the steps, I wrote in my notebook:

Exhibit A

THE 5 SALES STEPS

STEP 1: **KNOW THE PRODUCT**

Myself

STEP 2: **DEVELOP SALES TOOLS**

Resume

STEP 3: **DEVELOP PROSPECT LIST**

Where would I like to work
and who would need my skills

STEP 4: **SALES CALL**

Set an appointment and con-
duct the interview

STEP 5: **CLOSE**

Ask for the job, negotiate the
salary, accept or reject

"I really like these sales steps, Jessica! You know me, I like to see an organized approach to a task. I think it always makes it feel more manageable. I am really excited about getting started! What's my homework assignment?"

"We know that the first step in the sales process is to know the product, and, as I already explained, you are the product we are talking about. So, your first homework assignment is to learn as much as you can about yourself: your skills, your strengths, and your interests. To get at this information, I suggest you write down at least 10 achievements of which you are really proud. They can come from both your professional and private life and can go back as far as your childhood or be as current as today. For instance, an achievement of which I am very proud is that when I was a young girl I sold more Girl Scout Cookies than anyone in my brownie troop. (That sure was a glimpse into the future, wasn't it!) Not only do I want you to write down the accomplishment, but also the skills and personal qualities you think you needed in order to achieve these accomplishments. Give this exercise great consideration. The key to what you would like to do and what you are good at doing is found in the past."

"I'm really anxious to get started!"

"Good!" I am glad you feel so positive about this. You go home and do your homework and we can meet at The Blue Berry in the morning for breakfast to go over it, and then we will continue training at my house. Does 9:00 a.m. sound okay?"

* * *

*"The key to what you
would like to do and
what you are good at
is found in the past."*

* * *

"It sounds perfect. Thanks, again Jessica. I really appreciate this. You are a wonderful friend. I think if you hadn't reacted to my situation in such a helpful way, I'd probably be at home in my robe sobbing and feeling very sorry for myself. Instead, I feel excited and optimistic about the future. I hope someday I will be able to return the favor."

"It really is my pleasure, Beth. Of all the things I do, my favorite is teaching a novice the art of selling. So I am really getting a lot of enjoyment out of this."

"I can tell how much you enjoy talking about sales by the enthusiasm in your voice. I hope that I will find a job that I enjoy as much as you enjoy sales and sales training."

"Well, that's our goal, and when you do, you will hear that enthusiasm in your voice too. You should get home and get started on your homework."

"Yes, I'd better. It's been a long day. Dinner is on me, Jessica. I'll see you at nine o'clock."

Before you continue . . .

In your Job Success Notebook, write down ten achievements of which you are really proud. Remember, these achievements can come from either your professional or your private life and can go back as far as your childhood or be as current as today. Also, list the skills and personal qualities you think you needed in order to complete these achievements.

As a separate assignment, it would be beneficial for you to spend some time identifying your personal goal. What would you like to have or attain that will motivate you in your job search (i.e. a new car, a bigger house, membership at a health club, more education, etc.). Write your goal on the first page of your Job Success Notebook. Gather any material you can about it (brochures, books, pictures, etc.), and put it in your Notebook. Make your goal as real as possible.

Chapter Three

SECRET STEP 1—
DISCOVER YOUR
SKILLS AND ABILITIES

I heard the alarm go off and punched the snooze bar. I never get up at 7:30 on a Saturday morning, I thought as I rolled over and snuggled under my quilt. In spite of it being June in St. Louis, the nights were still cooling down to the low 60's which made for perfect sleeping weather. I laid there thinking of the events of the previous day and my upcoming weekend with Jessica. I had been up past midnight working on my achievements and skills homework assignment. When Jessica told me about it I thought it would be so simple, but when I actually did it, I found it was easier to remember all the things I did wrong in my life than to remember what I had done right.

The alarm sounded again telling me my five minutes of daydreaming time was up. I reluctantly pulled back the quilt and moved myself into the shower. The water felt good against my skin as it brought me to an awakened state. I dressed, got my homework together, and started out to The Blue Berry.

Even though the temperature was supposed to go up to 80, the morning air was still cool. It filled me with energy and optimism. I really need to get up and out early more often on the weekends, I thought.

I pulled up to The Blue Berry exactly at 9:00 o'clock and spotted Jessica's car in the parking lot. I went in and found Jessica looking over the vast array of muffins and Danish in the display case.

"Good morning, Jessica," I said.

"Good morning, Beth. This all looks so delicious, I never know what to choose."

"I know," I said. "Since this place opened, I have probably gained five pounds. It draws me here like a magnet about three times a week."

We both ordered a muffin and coffee at the bakery counter and found a booth to sit down in.

"How did your homework go, Beth?"

"It was much harder than I thought it would be. Why is it that we take so little notice of our achievements?"

"I don't know," replied Jessica. "but you are not alone in finding it a difficult task. I did this for myself not too long ago, and I also found it surprisingly difficult."

"That reminds me of something I was wondering about last night. How did you learn so much about job hunting?"

"You know how I have been telling you about a man named Sandy that I've been dating?"

"Yes. You sound like you are pretty fond of him."

"I am," Jessica smiled. "Well, Sandy is a career counselor. He does what you and I are going to do this weekend for a living; he helps people get their careers on track. We have had many conversations about career counseling, and I think it is a fascinating field. Funny enough though, when I first started dating Sandy, I didn't know what a career counselor was. I thought it was someone who found people jobs."

"That's what I thought it was too."

"We were both wrong. Career counselors help people evaluate what they have done in their jobs: what skills they have developed, where their strengths and interests are, and what career options they have. Then they help them develop marketing techniques so that they can go out and find good jobs on their own. The more Sandy talked about it, the more I saw a correlation between looking for a job and sales. Sandy and I have talked at great length about this connection, and he fully agrees. In fact, we came up with a whole program based on the theory. I gave you the outline last night. Sandy has been using the program very successfully in his practice, and now, I am going to use it with you."

"It sounds like you and Sandy have learned a lot from each other. Are you serious about him?" I asked as I finished off the last bite of my banana nut muffin.

"Yes, I am, and you will get a chance to see why. I told Sandy what we are doing this weekend and he asked if he could make dinner for us and see how we were coming along. I told him I would check with you first, and, if you have no objections, I will call him and let him know we would love to be his guests."

"Sounds great to me."

"Good, I think you will really like him. Also, he is truly one of the most objective people I know, and I think his opinion of what we are doing will be very valuable. I'll go call him and let him know we are coming, and I'll get us refills on coffee while I'm up."

As Jessica went to call Sandy and refill our cups at the self-serve coffee bar, I got out my homework and took a look at the achievements and skills I had formulated:

1. Came into an office where notification letters and filing were backed up eight weeks and had everything caught up within four weeks.

   Skills: organization

2. Increased staff and reorganized and expanded office space.

   Skills: Persuasion

3. Processed more loans in one month than any individual had done in the history of the company.

   Skills: hard work, diligence

4. Built strong relationships between field personnel, contractors, title, and insurance companies.

   Skills: good communication skills

5. Developed and wrote training manual for new personnel.

   Skills: creativity, writing

6. Coordinated meetings between sales staff and executives of company.

   Skills: organization, communications

7. Presented new materials to support staff on monthly basis.

   Skills: organization, ability to talk in front of a group

8. Assessed customer problems, proposed possible solutions, and carried through with customer.

   Skills: public relations, problem solving

9. Managed office of eight employees under difficult circumstances.

   Skills: management

10. Coordinated loan closings with buyer, title companies, insurance companies, mortgage companies and clients without ever having to postpone a closing.

    Skills: organization, communication, record keeping

As I looked the list over, I wondered how it could have possibly taken me three hours to come up with it. It all seemed pretty insignificant. I didn't discover a cure for some horrible disease or a new computer program that would revolutionize business. I didn't run a company or manage hundreds of people. I had only had two jobs and this was the sum of it all.

Jessica returned with two cups of steaming coffee.

"Is that your homework?" she asked.

"Yes," I said. "Nothing very exciting, I'm afraid."

"Let's see."

I handed over my homework feeling rather embarrassed.

Jessica read it over and said, "This looks fine, Beth. I don't know what you are feeling upset about. The only thing I notice beside the fact that you give yourself little credit for your skills is that you don't have any personal accomplishments on your list."

"Unlike you, Jessica, the only thing I did when I was a young girl was take care of my sick mother."

"How old were you, Beth?"

"I was 12 when she got sick and 16 when she died."

"Well, it seems to me you took on more responsibility than I did selling cookies. I know adults who can't take care of a sick parent! That must have taken great fortitude. I think it says a lot about you, Beth. Just as my cookie sales was a glimpse into my future, your ability to accept responsibility of a sick parent in what had to be a difficult situation was a glimpse into yours."

"Jessica, you always make me feel better."

"And you are always too hard on yourself! Now, let's look at the achievements on your list. Last night after we left Reuben's, I went by Sandy's and picked up some material for us to use. Sandy developed a Skills Word List that will be helpful to us in analyzing your achievements."

I watched Jessica open her well organized brief case.

"Let's look this over together," she said as she put the list on the table.

Exhibit B

SKILLS WORD LIST

administering
  programs
advising people
analyzing data
analyzing profit/loss
analyzing problems
appraising services
arranging social
  functions
articulating
  information
assembling machinery
assessing results
attending to detail
auditing records
calculating data
checking for accuracy
classifying records
coaching individuals
collecting money
communicating
  effectively
communicating with
  management
competing with others
compiling statistics
constructing structures

consulting with others
coordinating events
corresponding with
  others
counseling people
creating ideas
dealing with the
  public
delegating
  responsibility
designing systems
developing budgets
developing and
  designing products
developing and
  executing plans
developing
  educational
  programs
developing rapport
directing activities
directing people
directing operations
displaying artistic
  ideas
distributing products
editing materials

entertaining people
estimating space
evaluating programs
executing plans
facilitating meetings
following through
handling complaints
identifying/evaluating
  problems
implementing
  programs
initiating activities
inspecting situations
instilling enthusiasm
interfacing with
  executives
interpreting behavior
interpreting languages
interviewing people
inventing ideas
investigating problems
leading employees
listening
  empathetically
locating information
maintaining quality
making profit
making decisions
making presentations
managing people
managing territories

managing time
marketing
mediating
meeting deadlines
meeting people
monitoring progress of
  others
motivating people
negotiating
  agreements
operating personal
  computers
organizing work
overcoming obstacles
persuading others
planning agendas
planning activities
predicting problems
preparing financial
  statements
preparing materials
prioritizing needs
processing documents
programming
  computers
promoting products
promoting events
protecting property
providing advice and
  counsel
questioning others

raising funds
recording data
recruiting people
rehabilitating people
repairing mechanical
   machinery
researching
   information
researching products
resolving customer
   dissatisfaction
responding quickly
reviewing programs
selling
   products/services
sensing the needs of
   others
setting and attaining
   goals
solving problems

speaking in public
supervising others
surpassing quotas
taking charge
teaching
thinking logically
training
troubleshooting
understanding
   behavior
updating files
using spreadsheets
using talents of
   other people
visualizing ideas
working with a team
working with attention
   to detail
writing reports
writing creatively

My eyes started reading through the list. "I've done a lot of these things!" I said, somewhat amazed.

"I know you have, Beth. But when you analyzed your list you did what most people do, you used umbrella words like organize or communicate, rather than breaking it down to even more specific terms such as those on this list. Rather than just reading the list, I want you to write down all the skills that you think apply to your achievement list. We will be using this list later."

I turned to a clean page in my notebook and wrote:

1. Administering programs
2. Advising people
3. Analyzing problems
4. Appraising services
5. Attending to detail
6. Communicating with management
7. Coordinating events
8. Corresponding with others
9. Creating ideas
10. Dealing with the public
11. Developing & executing plans
12. Developing educational programs
13. Dispensing information
14. Facilitating meetings
15. Following-up
16. Identifying & evaluating problems
17. Implementing programs
18. Interfacing with executives

19. Interviewing people
20. Investigating problems
21. Leading employees
22. Listening actively
23. Making decisions
24. Making presentations
25. Managing operations
26. Operating personal computers
27. Organizing work
28. Overcoming obstacles
29. Persuading others
30. Prioritizing needs
31. Processing documents
32. Resolving customer dissatisfaction
33. Responding quickly
34. Reviewing programs
35. Scheduling programs
36. Solving problems
37. Supervising others
38. Taking charge
39. Teaching classes
40. Thinking logically
41. Updating files
42. Visualizing ideas

"Wow, Jessica, it looks like I have a lot more skills than I thought."

"I'd say so! You had listed 12 different skills in your homework as compared to the 42 that you got from the list, and all of these are legitimate, marketable, skills. By the

* * *

*"... a skill is a
skill whether you get
paid for using it or not."*

* * *

way, is there a reason you didn't list organizing that fund-raiser for the Women's Health Organization in your achievements? I thought you did an excellent job!"

"I didn't think something I did as a volunteer would be very significant."

"A lot of people have that same thought. But, remember, a skill is a skill whether you get paid for using it or not."

"Well, that was a successful event, wasn't it. We raised more money on that event than any other one the organization had previously sponsored."

"Looking at the skills list, are there any additional skills you used for this event?"

I scanned the list again. "Yes, I would add:

1. Arranging social functions
2. Executing plans
3. Instilling enthusiasm (in volunteers)
4. Promoting events
5. Raising funds

"Wow, Jessica, that brings the list to 47. Now, if I could get $1,000 per year per skill, I'd be in good shape!"

"Wishful thinking, Beth. I'm afraid it doesn't work that way. But you certainly will be in a better position to market yourself at a higher value if you know and can present all the skills you bring to the job. There is one thing I would like to point out, though, and that is on your original skill list you wrote hard work and diligence as your skills for achievement #3. Those are really qualities you have but not skills. Good personal qualities are also important to an employer. Here is a list of personal qualities Sandy has prepared. You should go through it and know which ones you would want to be able to point out when you are in an interview. Remember, you don't want to confuse those personal qualities with your skills. Just to be clear, let me define each word for you. I looked them up when I went through this exercise with Sandy. Skill means ability and proficiency; an art, trade, or technique. Quality means an inherent or distinguishing characteristic, a personal trait. So if we go back and look at the skills you used in processing more loans in one month than any individual had done in the history of the company, the skills I would think you used would have been your computer skills and organizational skills, as well as your ability to process documents, prioritize needs, and attend to detail etc. Those skills plus the personal qualities you listed allowed you to get the job done. Does this make sense to you?

Exhibit C

Qualities Word List

adaptable
adept
analytical
articulate
artistic
astute
capable
caring
commanding
compassionate
competent
competitive
composed
concerned
concise
confident
conscientious
conservative
considerate
convincing
cool-headed
cooperative
creative
decisive
detail oriented
determined

discriminating
dynamic
economical
effective
efficient
empathic
energetic
entertaining
enthusiastic
fact-minded
flexible
forceful
forward thinking
goal oriented
good natured
handy
hardworking
imaginative
independent
innovative
inquisitive
inspiring
intelligent
intuitive
inventive
knowledgeable

level headed
logical
objective
observant
open-minded
patient
people oriented
persistent
persuasive
practical
pragmatic
precise
principles
productive
proficient
quiet

realistic
reflective
reliable
resourceful
result oriented
safety conscious
serious minded
tactful
team oriented
technical
thorough
understanding
versatile
warm
wise

"Yes, it's very clear," I said as my eyes scanned the Qualities Word list. "I never thought about distinguishing between skills and qualities, but it certainly makes sense. I will remember it. What's next?"

"Next, I want you to go over your list of 47 skills and give them a number value from one to ten: ten being the skill you would like to use the most and feel you are good at and one being the skill you feel is weakest and/or you least like to use."

I took the list and started rating them. "This is fun," I said as I moved through the list. Within five minutes I was done.

1. Administering programs	8
2. Advising people	5
3. Analyzing problems	8
4. Appraising services	6
5. Attending to detail	2
6. Communicating with management	5
7. Coordinating events	8
8. Corresponding with others	8
9. Creating ideas	10
10. Dealing with the public	10
11. Developing & executing plans	10
12. Developing educational programs	3
13. Dispensing information	2
14. Facilitating meetings	5
15. Following through	4
16. Identifying & evaluating problems	8
17. Implementing programs	6

18. Interfacing with executives	5
19. Interviewing people	9
20. Investigating problems	10
21. Leading employees	3
22. Listening actively	7
23. Making decisions	8
24. Making presentations	5
25. Managing operations	2
26. Operating personal computers	8
27. Organizing work	6
28. Overcoming obstacles	5
29. Persuading others	8
30. Prioritizing needs	8
31. Processing documents	8
32. Resolving customer dissatisfaction	10
33. Responding quickly	9
34. Reviewing programs	4
35. Scheduling programs	5
36. Solving problems	8
37. Supervising others	4
38. Taking charge	9
39. Teaching classes	8
40. Thinking logically	7
41. Updating files	1
42. Visualizing ideas	8
43. Arranging social functions	6
44. Executing plans	8
45. Instilling enthusiasm (in volunteers)	6
46. Promoting events	8
47. Raising funds	5

"You certainly seem to know what you like and what you don't like doing." Jessica said as she flashed her contagious smile.

"Yes, I guess I do at that," I responded.

"What I'd like you to do now is write all your Tens in a column, then your Nines and then your Eights."

"O.K.," I said as I wrote:

Tens

Creating ideas
Dealing with the public
Developing and Executing plans
Investigating problems
Resolving customer dissatisfaction

Nines

Interviewing people
Responding quickly
Taking charge

Eights

Administering programs
Analyzing problems
Coordinating events
Corresponding with others

Identifying and evaluating problems
Making decisions
Operating personal computers
Persuading others
Prioritizing needs
Processing documents
Solving problems
Visualizing ideas
Executing plans
Promoting events

"This is really interesting, Beth. I am sure you notice a pattern here of skills that complement each other. If you look at some of your Tens such as creating ideas and investigating problems, and then look down your list of Eights, you see many of the Eights actually support what you believe to be your best skills."

I scanned my list of Eights and saw analyzing problems, identifying and evaluating problems, solving problems, and visualizing ideas. I looked again at my Tens, and I realized exactly what Jessica meant, the same skills were in both lists.

"Most people who do this exercise will be able to see a similar pattern. Based on these patterns, we can go to step 2, developing the sales tools."

"You mean I finished step one?" I asked excitedly.

"Yes. I think you have clearly defined the skills you are good at and the ones you would most like to use. In addition,

I think you will agree that you know yourself (in terms of job skills) much better than you did when we started last night."

"I definitely agree with you there. When we first started, I had no clear idea of the skills I had been using. I am already feeling much more confident about my abilities."

"Good," Jessica said. "Now I suggest we go back to my apartment where we can spread out our materials and be more comfortable. Then we'll go into the next step which will be to develop your marketing tools."

Before you continue . . .

Turn back to the Skills List and take out your achievement list. In your Job Success Notebook, write down all the skills that you think you used to accomplish your achievements. Once you have written your list, go back and give them a number value from one to ten: ten being the skill you would like to use the most and feel you are good at, and one being the skill you feel is weakest and/or you least like to use. Now, put all the skills numbered eight, nine and ten on one sheet of paper.

It would also be to your benefit to look at the qualities list and write down the personal qualities you believe you possess.

As soon as you complete this exercise, please congratulate yourself. You have finished secret step one!

Chapter Four

SECRET STEP 2—
WRITE A FUTURE
ORIENTED RESUME

As I drove to Jessica's apartment, I felt a great sense of accomplishment. I had finished step one! I was as proud of myself as I had been when I finished the weekend computer class at the Junior College. I was anxious to start step two and see what would develop. What's so exciting about this, I thought, is you don't know exactly what's going to come out until it happens.

I drove up to Jessica's apartment right behind her and followed her in.

"Jessica, I love your apartment! It's so cheerful and modern." Jessica's apartment had mauve carpeting on which she had a large white sofa and chair with throw pillows in mauve, white, pink, peach and teal Monet style flowers, brass and glass tables, white torch lamps, and an entertainment center with beveled mirroring and brass trim. In the dining room she had a long glass table with four chairs upholstered to match the throw pillows. Along the back wall were two sliding glass doors that led to a deck built into a very natural setting of trees and a little stream. Jessica had lovely pots of petunias, impatiences, geraniums and ferns sitting all around the deck along with two white chaise lounges.

"I love this apartment too," Jessica said. "The builders did such a good job of leaving the natural setting. It's wonderful to come home after a stressful day and sit on the deck and listen to the birds and the trickling water in the stream. Within 20 minutes I feel calm and at peace. Maybe you could move here too, Beth, when your lease is up."

"I'd love to if I could afford it."

"Well, it might be a nice goal for you to shoot for."

"I'll say. I think I could get pretty motivated if I thought I could afford to live in this beautiful setting."

"Good! Goals are supposed to be motivating. I make my sales trainees write out their goals. When we take a break we can go over to the leasing office and get a price list. They have about five different floor plans, and each one is priced differently. If this is really where you would like to live, then make it your goal. It can be a short term goal or a long term goal. It doesn't matter which as long as you keep working toward it.

"If we are going to get you to your goal, we had better start working. Let's sit down at the dining room table so we can spread out all our paperwork. Step two involves developing marketing tools which in your case, as with the majority of people, will be a resume."

"Oh no! I hate writing resumes!" I said with a sinking feeling.

"You and the rest of the world. Sometimes I think people stay in jobs they hate just so they won't have to write a resume. That's why this sales system we are using works so well. Believe it or not, you almost have your resume written."

"Really?" I said amazed.

"Really. Get out your notebook and turn to the last list that you did where you listed all the Ten's, Nines, and Eights."

I did as Jessica told me to and laid my list on the dining room table. Jessica opened her brief case and took out some material. She looked through it and then pulled a sheet out and laid it next to my list.

"Here is the format for your resume," she said. "Basically, you already have all the answers we need; we just have to fill in the blanks starting with your career objective."

Exhibit D
RESUME FORMAT

NAME
ADDRESS
PHONE NUMBER

CAREER OBJECTIVE

A position utilizing my skills and abilities including:

-
-
-

resulting in...

QUALIFICATIONS

Qualified by experience encompassing:

-
-
-

ACHIEVEMENTS

-
-
-

EXPERIENCE

EDUCATION

I looked the sheet over. "This looks simple enough, but I don't understand what you want. We never really discussed my career objective."

"You are right, Beth. We didn't discuss your career objective, at least we didn't call it that. But doesn't it make sense that your career objective would be one where you could use the skills you rated as Nines and Tens?"

"Yes, It sounds like a utopia, but don't I have to put as my career objective a very specific title like Office Manager, Public Relations Representative, etc.?"

"No, you don't. In fact, putting a title down on your resume is really something you want to avoid. It assumes that all organizations will use the same titles, which is certainly not true. For example, in sales, different companies title their sales people differently. They may call them Account Managers, Account Executives, Service Representatives, and so forth. In addition, a specific title can be limiting. Often people go to an interview for one position and in the process discover there is also another position open. This opening may be even better than the one they originally went to interview for. If they put a specific title down on their resume, the interviewer may not even consider them for the other opening. For instance, I bet you would make a great Events Planner, and I'll bet you never even heard of that title."

"You're right. I never heard of an Events Planner, what is it?"

"I just know a little bit about it because one of my sales representatives has a sister who is an Events Planner for a large corporation, and he was telling me what she does. In fact, he was suggesting that perhaps our company could use one. Apparently, an Events Planner is a person who works for a company or perhaps a non-profit or educational institution and plans their events. This could include seminars, sales meetings, company retreats, picnics and dinners, athletic events, fund raisers, etc. If you think of large national or international companies, they must have numerous activities throughout the year. I know our company does. The Events Planner arranges everything, coordinating travel plans, rooms, caterers, invitations, podiums, sound systems, decorations, etc. Everything that would be included in that event."

"That sounds fascinating! Do you really think I could do that?"

"Yes, I think it would use many of your highly rated skills. But our job right now is not to determine exactly what you could do with your skills, but to develop a resume that will give you as wide a range as possible from which to choose. Is this still making sense to you?"

"Yes, and it's so exciting! Thank you, Jessica. I can't tell you how much I appreciate all you've taught me since we

* * *

*"... our job right now
is not to determine exactly
what you could do with
your skills, but to
develop a resume that
will give you as wide
a range as possible
from which to
choose."*

* * *

started this. I never heard of approaching a new job in this manner."

"I never did either until I met Sandy."

"I am really looking forward to meeting him. What time is he expecting us for dinner?"

"We'll go over about six. I think he is going to barbecue."

"Where does Sandy live?"

"About a block away. He's in the complex. In fact, I first met him at the swimming pool. I would like Sandy to see your resume when we go over tonight, so we better get working. The first thing we need to determine is your career objective. Take out a clean piece of paper and we will follow the resume outline Sandy developed and fill in the appropriate information."

I tore a clean sheet of paper out of my notebook and wrote:

Career Objective

A position utilizing my skills and abilities including:

I looked at the skills that I had rated as Tens. "Should I put all five of my top rated skills in, Jessica?"

"It's up to you. You can use all five here or we can include some in the qualifications. Remember, you are the product we are selling. What features do you want to emphasize the most?"

I looked at the list again. These are hard choices, I thought, but I guess I better start somewhere. I really like developing and executing plans, creating ideas and dealing with the public. I also think I am extremely good at resolving customer problems. I just seem to have a knack for calming people down and communicating with them—I think it comes from the Active Listening class I took. So, for career objective I am going to write:

- Developing and Executing Plans
- Creating Ideas
- Communicating with the Public
- Resolving Customer and/or Company Problems

Jessica watched me as I wrote. "Good, Beth. You are a fifth of the way there. Now, when you bring these skills to an employer how are they going to benefit the company? In sales, whenever we give a feature, we always follow up with a benefit. Like, use this detergent; it will get your clothes whiter than white."

"I understand. For myself I would say: Because I can create, develop, and execute plans, I can work very independently. The company can give me a project and I will run with it. It can involve working with people internally or with the public."

"Okay, that sounds good," said Jessica. "But we need to boil it down to about one sentence. If you have one sentence to say how you can benefit a company using your skills, what would that sentence be. Remember, start your sentence with 'resulting in.' Here, look at this Action Words List Sandy developed. Maybe it will help generate the kernel you are trying to get to. The list will also help you in writing your achievements."

Exhibit E

ACTION WORDS LIST

accelerated	attained	completed
accepted	attracted	composed
accomplished	audited	computed
accounted	authored	conceived
achieved	averted	conceptualized
acquired	awarded	concluded
acted	bargained	conducted
activated	bought	conferred
adapted	briefed	confined
addressed	built	consolidated
adjusted	calculated	constructed
administered	campaigned	consulted
adopted	cataloged	contracted
advanced	centralized	contributed
advised	certified	controlled
affected	charted	converted
analyzed	checked	cooperated
anticipated	clarified	coordinated
applied	classified	corrected
appointed	coached	corresponded
appraised	collaborated	counseled
arbitrated	collected	created
arranged	combined	critiqued
assembled	communicated	cut
assessed	compared	decentralized
assisted	compiled	decided

decreased	enforced	handled
defined	enhanced	harmonized
delegated	enlarged	headed
delivered	enlightened	helped
demonstrated	entrusted	hired
designed	established	identified
detailed	estimated	illuminated
detected	evaluated	illustrated
determined	examined	implemented
developed	exceeded	improved
devised	exchanged	improvised
diagnosed	executed	increased
directed	expanded	indexed
discovered	expedited	influenced
dispensed	explained	informed
displayed	explored	initiated
disproved	facilitated	innovated
disseminated	filed	inspected
distributed	followed	inspired
diverted	through	installed
documented	forecasted	instituted
doubled	formed	instructed
drafted	formulated	integrated
economized	fostered	interacted
edited	founded	interceded
effected	funneled	interpreted
eliminated	gathered	interviewed
employed	governed	introduced
enabled	graphed	invented
encouraged	guided	inventoried

investigated	optimized	recruited
issued	ordered	rectified
judged	organized	reduced
justified	originated	referred
launched	overhauled	refined
learned	oversaw	regulated
lectured	packaged	reinforced
led	painted	rejected
located	participated	related
logged	perceived	removed
made	performed	rendered
maintained	persuaded	renegotiated
managed	pioneered	reorganized
marketed	planned	repaired
maximized	positioned	replaced
measured	prepared	reported
mediated	presided	represented
met	prevented	researched
minimized	procured	reshaped
moderated	produced	resolved
modernized	programmed	responded
modified	publicized	restored
monitored	published	retrieved
motivated	purchased	revamped
navigated	raised	reversed
negotiated	realized	reviewed
observed	received	revised
obtained	recommended	revitalized
offered	reconciled	routed
operated	recorded	safeguarded

saved	strengthened	transacted
scheduled	structured	translated
screened	studied	traveled
secured	suggested	treated
separated	summarized	triggered
served	supervised	trimmed
serviced	supplied	tutored
set	supported	undertook
settled	surveyed	unified
shaped	symbolized	united
sought	synthesized	upgraded
specified	systematized	used
spoke	tabulated	utilized
staffed	taught	validated
standardized	terminated	varied
started	tested	verified
stimulated	took charge	weighed
straightened	traded	won
streamlined	trained	worked
		wrote

My mind felt like it was on overdrive, straining to get up a mountain. My eyes looked down the list and the thoughts began to form as I wrote:

resulting in improved efficiency, organization, and administration of company programs

"Very good!" Jessica said, as I transferred the sentence onto the appropriate place on the resume. "Next we need to put in your qualifications. In other words, what can you say that shows you are qualified for your career objective. You might want to look at the Action Word List again as well as the skills you rated with Eights and Nines. Remember, we are starting this section out with 'Qualified by successful experience encompassing...'

"I'll go get us some tea and a snack while you work on your qualifications."

I sat there in Jessica's cheerful dining room looking out the sliding glass door into the trees. Why am I qualified, I thought, and in my notebook I wrote: I am qualified by successful experience encompassing... Certainly I should put administrating policies and procedures. My eyes kept scanning the three lists in front of me: the Skills list, the Action Words list, and my Eight through Ten skill list. All the while I felt my mind racing back through the work I had done, trying to coordinate my work to these lists. As it all was churning together, I wrote:

- Administrating policies and procedures
- Making decisions
- Handling complaints
- Identifying and evaluating needs
- Developing and implementing programs

I finished transferring the list onto my resume as Jessica returned with a tray containing tea, crackers, cheese, and fresh strawberries.

"Thanks, Jessica, this looks wonderful! What time is it?"

"Believe it or not, it's already 1:30. What we are doing now takes a lot of thought. It looks like we are about half way there, though. Let me see what you put."

I handed Jessica my resume as I sipped on the hot tea and took a bite of cheese and cracker. "This tastes wonderful, Jessica. Thinking always makes me hungry!"

"It's paying off, Beth. Your resume is really shaping up. The next section, achievements, shouldn't be too hard because you already have them written out. Why don't you pick out the five or six that you would like to highlight. It would be good if you would add on to the end of each achievement what it resulted in. In other words, show that you were effective. Companies want proven success. But, before you start, I think we could use a fifteen minute break. Would you like to walk up to the clubhouse now?"

"Yes, that sounds like fun."

We finished our snack, took the dishes into Jessica's white, butler style kitchen and went outside. The apartment unit was beautifully landscaped and well kept. "How many apartments are there, Jessica?" I asked.

"Oh, I think around 300 units including townhouses. It's a pretty big complex."

We went by the pool and came to the entrance of the clubhouse. The inside was as modern as Jessica's apartment.

"Hi, Jessica," said one of the office personnel.

"Hi, Ruth. How are things going?"

"Busy as ever. What can we do for you?"

"This is my friend, Beth. She is thinking of moving here, and I wanted to get her diagrams of the floor plans and a cost sheet."

"Hi, Beth," the woman said to me with a smile. "Let me get you the information."

She went to a file drawer and pulled out a ready made packet. "This should tell you everything you want to know," she said. "After you have looked it over, please feel free to call me if you have any questions. I hope we will see you here. I know we look big, but we try to make it feel warm and comfortable."

"And, you do a great job!" said Jessica. "Thanks, Ruth."

"Nice meeting you," I said as I took the packet. We walked back to Jessica's and I put the packet with my job notes, thinking how much fun it would be later to look at all the information. It would be my special treat for all the work I was doing with Jessica.

"Jessica, I think you took me up there to inspire me into a grand finale on this resume."

"Well, we can all use a little boost every now and then, and I believe in visualizing goals. I want you to see yourself in the apartment; think about where you will put the furniture. I must say this is not a new thought. All great sales trainers believe in visualizing goals. Are you ready to finish your resume now?"

"You bet! I went back through my notebook and found the pages with my achievements and read through them again. I wrote down in my notebook:

- Assessed customer problems, and proposed and implemented solutions resulting in the lowest level of customer complaints in five years.

- Created, organized and executed plans for fund raising event resulting in highest level of contributions in organization's history.

- Built strong relationships between field personnel, contractors, mortgage bankers and insurance companies resulting in work being finished on or before schedule and increased company profits.

- Increased and reorganized staff and work space resulting in a more efficient and productive office with the ability to handle a substantially higher volume of business.

- Processed more loans in one month than any individual in the history of the company.

"Jessica, I think the result for the last achievement is self evident. What do you think?"

Jessica looked over my list and said, "I agree. Sometimes it doesn't fit to put results in. Having a little mixture like this is fine. You do want to rank the achievements in order starting with the one you feel was most important, though."

"I guess I just did it naturally."

"Good. After you transfer these to your resume, we are truly coming down the home stretch. All we need is your experience and education."

I wrote the achievements onto my resume and said to Jessica, "What do people do who don't have achievements from their work, like college students or homemakers going back to work?"

"Good question. I asked Sandy the same thing. He said they have to rely on achievements in school or volunteer work. Remember what I said earlier, you don't have to be paid for something to make it a significant and marketable achievement. Now, what about your experience?"

"Experience is easy. I worked for two companies, Sureco Development Company and Pacific Mortgage Insurance Company. I'm not sure I remember the months, but I remember the years."

"That's fine. Putting in the months really is not necessary. But do put in the titles you had at each company."

I wrote on my resume:

Experience:

Pacific Mortgage Insurance Company   1991-1992
   ■ Office Manager

Sureco Development Company   1983-1991
   ■ Loan Officer
   ■ Assistant Loan Officer
   ■ Department Secretary

"I never know what to put for education, Jessica. I have over two years of college credits plus other training seminars but no degree. I know it keeps me from getting many jobs I think I am qualified for."

"I know, Beth. It's a real problem for bright, talented people like yourself, and often it isn't fair, but all you can do is try to overcome it. Some companies will be open to you and some will only see you in support positions. Since you have less than three years of college, I suggest you put your college experience without dates and list any training seminars that relate to the type of work you would like to do under a separate heading."

I wrote on my resume:

Education
- University of Missouri
- Liberal Arts

Seminars
- Personal Computers and Business Software
- Effective Listening

"Jessica, don't you think I should put something on the resume under Personal?"

"It really isn't necessary, and in your case I don't see an advantage. Employers are scared by divorced, single mothers. They are afraid you will lose work time taking care of the children if they are sick. I also think they still look at divorced people as unreliable. All in all, I don't see anything for you to gain by putting that information down. The opposite may hold true for people who are married. Some employers will interpret marriage as indicating more stability. However, I think women volunteering that they have young children will still send up a red flag, even if it's unconscious on the part of the employer. If two people are equal for the job, and one has young children to care for and the other doesn't, I think that could become a deciding factor. In the same vein, rarely is it a good idea to put in age. It's a no win situation. One person will think you are too young, and another will think you are too old. What do you think?"

"I think you are right. Why volunteer information that might make someone feel negatively toward me before they even meet me. Does that mean I'm done with my resume?"

"Yes, Beth. Believe it or not, you have finished your resume! Let's go into my office and I will put it on my computer for you. I have a program already set up using Sandy's form so it will only take me a few minutes."

"Thanks, Jessica. I am excited about seeing it in print, and I don't have a computer. What would I do if you weren't here to put it on your computer?"

"Fortunately, there are a lot of services available today at copy centers. You would take your hand printed or typewritten form to one of these centers, and they would use their computers and laser printers to set it up for you. Since I have a laser printer on my computer, you won't need to do this, but you will need to follow the next steps. Have a copy center make about 75 copies of the resume for you. (The quality is so good from the laser printer, that you really don't need to go to the expense of having the resume printed). Pick a colored paper for them to copy onto. I would suggest a vanilla color or light gray. You will also want to get plain sheets of paper in the same color with matching envelopes for cover letters and thank you letters."

I watched Jessica put my resume onto her computer and waited anxiously as her printer followed her command to print it out.

"Jessica, it looks wonderful!"

Exhibit F

BETH A. HOLSTER
6783B Hartley Dr.
St. Louis, MO 63130
(314)223-7818

CAREER OBJECTIVE

A position utilizing my skills and abilities including:
- Developing and Executing Plans
- Creating Ideas
- Communicating with the Public
- Resolving Customer and Company Problems

resulting in improved efficiency, organization, and administration of company programs.

QUALIFICATIONS

Qualified by experience encompassing:
- Making Decisions
- Handling Complaints
- Identifying and Evaluating Needs
- Developing and Implementing Programs
- Administrating Policies and Procedures

ACHIEVEMENTS

Assessed customer problems, proposed and implemented solutions resulting in lowest level of customer complaints in five years.

Created, organized and executed plans for fund raising event resulting in highest level of contributions in organization's history.

Built Strong Relationships between field personnel, contractors, mortgage bankers and insurance companies resulting in work being finished on or before schedule and increased company profits.

Increased and reorganized staff and work space resulting in a more efficient and productive office with ability to handle substantially higher volume of business.

Processed more loans in one month than any individual in the history of the company.

EXPERIENCE

Pacific Mortgage Insurance Company   1991-1992
- Office Manager

Sureco Development Company   1983-1991
- Loan Officer
- Assistant Loan Officer
- Department Secretary

EDUCATION

University of Missouri
- Liberal Arts

Seminars
- Personal Computers and Business Software
- Effective Listening

Before you continue . . .

Now it is time for you to write your resume. Please take your Eight through Ten skills list out of your Job Success Notebook and turn to a clean piece of paper. Open the book to the resume outline page, and write your resume. It may help to reread the parts of this chapter relating to writing the resume several times as you fill in the outline. Take your time! Your resume is an important sales tool!

When you have finished your resume, take it to a copy center that will format it on a computer and print it with a good laser printer. Choose the color paper you want and have them make 75 copies. Also get matching plain paper and envelopes for cover letters and thank you letters. The appearance of your resume and correspondence is important so don't try to save a few dollars by using an inferior type or paper. When you have finished your resume, don't forget to congratulate yourself. You have gotten over a major hump in the job search process, and you have also finished the second secret step!

Chapter Five

SECRET STEP 3—
IDENTIFY AND
APPROACH
THE MARKET

"I can't believe the wonderful sense of accomplishment each time I finish one of these steps, Jessica. But even more than that, every time we complete a step, I feel as though another heavy weight has been lifted from me."

"Maybe it's because we have all come to believe that there is practically nothing worse than writing a resume and looking for a job. No one ever explains the options or clearly and simply defines the process, and so we all stumble around in the dark and take any job just to end the agony. Unfortunately, what often happens is that six months into the new job, we find ourselves no happier than we were in the old job.

"Which brings us to examining where you would like to work and who could best use your skills."

"Wouldn't I just look at mortgage banking firms and commercial development companies?"

"Why? Beth."

"Because that's where I worked before."

"Your answer is the answer almost all people give. But, in truth, your options are definitely more far reaching than just these two areas. What we just did in your resume was to define your skills. These are skills used in many fields. They are what are called transferable, marketable skills. In other words, they transfer to other fields, and they are in demand (marketable). If you look at the skills you listed, administrating policies and procedures, making decisions, etc., I am sure you will agree that many companies need and use these skills."

"They sure do! But how would I begin? I can't go to every company in town. Anyway, don't I have to know that there is an opening?"

"Remember, we are following a sales system. Let me give

you an example. I sell computer software systems. My first step in the sale is to identify the companies who might use my product. Now, if I call these companies and say, 'Do you need computer software systems?' the chances are pretty great they will say, 'No, we already have enough systems in place,' or 'We can't afford it.' So my objective is not to find out if they need software, but just to get an appointment to show them my software and how my software would benefit their company. Once I do that, I will get one of three responses:

1. They didn't have a system—they like mine—they buy it (There is a need.)

2. They can see the advantage of my software in addition to what they have and will buy it. (I created a need.)

3. They are happy with what they have and are not interested. (Even here, I made a contact that may call me at a later time or may refer me to someone who has a need.)

"Now, when I make the appointment to go to the company, one thing is very critical to my sale and that is who I make the appointment with. I can go and talk with department managers and show them how my product will benefit their department. They may love it; they may want me to install it ASAP, BUT IF THEY ARE NOT THE DECISION MAKER CHANCES ARE GOOD IT WILL NEVER HAPPEN! Therefore, I only make appointments with decision makers: the people who have the authority to buy my product if they can see how it will benefit their company.

"The same holds true for people looking for a job. First, identify companies who could use your skills. Second, identify the decision maker in the company who would have the authority to hire you. Third, set up the appointment.

"Since your skills are very general, I suggest you start narrowing things down some by first identifying some career fields and industries that you would enjoy working in. A good tool for doing this is the want ads because the paper is set up by career fields and/or industries. Circle all the ads that sound interesting to you. Remember, you are not necessarily looking for a job at this point; you are just identifying career fields and industries you think you would enjoy. Also remember, you do not have to have 100% of the qualifications listed in an ad, including a college degree. Ads are always an employer's wish list of qualifications that their ideal candidate would have. It is very unlikely they will find someone with 100% of their list of qualifications.

"It's 4:00 p.m. Why don't you take about an hour for this, and while you are reading through the ads, I'm going to do some work in my office."

Jessica went to the front door, got the paper, and handed it to me. I opened it up and took out the classified ads. As Jessica instructed, I started at the beginning of the ads with A. Boy, there were some interesting jobs I would never have thought of had I not read every ad. Here was one for an Assistant Volunteer Coordinator at a hospital. It sounded something like an Events Coordinator. I definitely wanted to look into that! I guess I still liked banking, I thought as I read on and circled many of the banking ads. Public relations, these sounded interesting. I couldn't believe it! Here was an ad for a Special Events Assistant. Wait until I show Jessica, I thought. I certainly didn't have all the qualifications listed in the ad, but I circled it anyway.

Exhibit G—The Ad

SPECIAL EVENTS ASSISTANT

Cardinal Medical Center has an immediate full-time opening for a Special Events Assistant. Hours: Monday—Friday 8:00 a.m.—5:00 p.m. including weekends/evenings for events.

Duties include assisting in the planning of conferences, special events, seminars, and group tours of the Medical Center.

Requires a Bachelor's degree (Business, Communications or Hospitality). Absolute minimum full-time work experience of one—three years in meeting/special events planning. Experience in desktop publishing and computer necessary. Experience in Meeting Pro Software helpful.

Organizational and communication (oral and written) skills necessary. Must be flexible, energetic and willing to adjust personal schedule to accommodate work schedule.

Cardinal offers an excellent salary commensurate with experience including an excellent benefits package. For consideration, submit resume or apply in person.

Human Resources
CARDINAL MEDICAL CENTER
1212 South Fourth Street
Cardinal, MO 66666
Attn: Mary Combs

Equal Opportunity Employer

As I was finishing what seemed like the millionth sales ad promising $100,000 after six months, I heard Jessica's voice call out of her office, "Are you done yet?"

"Has it been an hour already?"

"It sure has."

"I can't believe it! Yes, I am almost done. Give me five more minutes."

"Okay, I'll call Sandy and see how things are going with dinner."

Jessica came out of her room as I finished the last ad.

"That was fascinating. I saw jobs and industries I didn't realize existed."

"Good!" Jessica smiled. "The next step is approaching the companies for a job. You can approach in two ways. One way is simply to answer any of the ads you circled in the paper where you were interested in the job. Another is to contact a decision maker in an industry you are interested in for what is called an informational interview. The job approach is pretty straight forward. You send your resume with a cover letter. Sandy showed me an excellent cover letter to use when answering ads in the paper. He calls it an 'I' letter because when it is done it looks like an 'I.' Here, he gave me some examples for you. As you can see, you want

81

to read the ad, determine what abilities and experience the employer is looking for, and coordinate your achievements and experience with what they want.

"Let's look at an example. Which ad would you like to respond to?"

"I found one for a Special Events Assistant."

"You're kidding! Well, let's look at it. Give me a piece of paper, and I'll write the letter with you. Obviously, we want to start out with a formal heading. Then we will have an introductory paragraph. Next, we will determine what abilities and experience are being asked for and match some of your skills and/or achievements with the requirements, and finally we will have a closing paragraph. So the finished letter might read:

Exhibit H

The "I" LETTER

August 1, 1993

Ms. Mary Combs
Cardinal Medical Center
1212 South Fourth Street
Cardinal, MO 66666

Dear Ms. Combs:

With skills and experience including creating ideas, developing and executing plans, and resolving problems, I am an excellent candidate for the Special Events Assistant. Below is a list of my qualifications as they relate to your requirements.

Minimum 3 years experience	Five years experience conferences/seminars planning and implementing effective conferences and seminars in a timely manner.
Computer experience	Macintosh and IBM personal computers. Word Perfect, Lotus 1-2-3 and other business software.
Oral/Written skills	Wrote and presented business reports at weekly staff meetings.
Flexible, energetic and willing to accommodate a changing work schedule	Processed more loans in one month than any individual in the history of the company by working any schedule necessary to be successful.

I have enclosed a resume for your review and look forward to meeting with you to discuss your opportunity and the contribution I can make. I will call you in a few days to set up a mutually convenient appointment.

Sincerely,

Beth A. Holester

Enclosure

"When you look at this you can see why Sandy calls it an 'I' letter."

"I certainly can. I also see why it would be more effective than a traditional letter. It's in such an unusual form, it makes you read it."

"Exactly! You have also given several positive examples of your skills.

"The request for an informational interview is the second type of approach, and it is a little more complicated than the 'I' letter. It is very important that you understand this type of approach because it opens up far more possibilities for jobs than just answering ads does. Everyone who is looking for a job reads the ads and sends a resume. Our company can get hundreds of resumes from one ad in the Sunday paper. So, obviously, competition from the ads is fierce.

"The informational interview gives you an opportunity to meet with a decision maker without all that competition. The decision maker knows information and movement in his or her company better than anyone. For example, a decision maker is aware of a promotion coming up or, on the other hand, a person about to be fired. Either situation will leave a vacancy. Decision makers are also aware of growth, which creates the need for additional personnel and even new departments. Most importantly, they are people who can actually create a position for someone if they are really impressed with the person's talents. Remember what I told you about how I will only give presentations to decision makers because they have the authority to buy my product if they see the need for it? Well, as we said when we started this process, you are now the product."

"But, Jessica, I don't know decision makers."

"Beth, you probably know more than you think. First of all, a decision maker can be someone whose name you know through business or whom you saw at a meeting or seminar. In other words, you don't have to know them well. Secondly, you can get names of decision makers from other people you know who are not decision makers themselves but come in contact with decision makers through their work. For instance, your insurance salesman or your tax preparer, your doctor, or someone in business, like me."

"Jessica, how can I ask my insurance man for names of decision makers."

"Really, Beth, it's simple. Just be honest. Tell him you are currently on a career campaign and you are trying to get information about the health care field, for example. Could he give you the names of any decision makers he knows in that field that you could approach for information. You might add that you are not going to embarrass him by asking this person for a job, you are only trying to get information about the career field. That usually will put the person more at ease about giving out names.

"The third way to get names of decision makers is through research. Articles in local newspapers and magazines, local or national publications like Dun and Bradstreet (the reference librarian at the library would be a good source for the name of local publications), and the company itself. For example, you can call straight into a company and ask the receptionist, 'Could you give me the name of your public relations director?' Usually, the receptionist will not hesitate to give you a name.

"Ask! Ask! Ask! The worst people can do is say no!

"Now, we'll assume you have the names and titles of several decision makers you have identified in fields in which you are interested. Fifteen to twenty-five would be a good number to aim for. The first step to the appointment is writing them a letter asking for the interview. This type of letter is called the Approach Letter. Here is a sample of one from Sandy."

Exhibit I

THE APPROACH LETTER

November 6, 1993

John Smith
Director of Development
Applebee, Inc.
1111 Pear Street
Cardinal, MO 66666

Dear John:

Ellen Jackson referred me to you. I am currently on a career campaign. My objective is a career position where I can utilize my proven people skills as well as my ability to create, organize, and execute internal and external programs.

I would appreciate the opportunity to meet with you for 15 or 20 minutes to share information about your field and get your opinion as to whether or not my career objective is realistic. I do not expect you to have a position available or know of one.

I have enclosed my resume so that you may have a better idea of my background. I will call you on Wednesday to set up a mutually convenient time.

Let me thank you in advance for any information or advice you may share with me.

I look forward to meeting with you.

Sincerely,

Martha Washington
8214 Heritage Street
Cardinal, MO 66656
(314) 111-2121

encl.

***

"ASK! ASK! ASK!
The worst people
can do is say no!"

***

"As you can see, you want to start out by mentioning a few of your strengths. You want to go on to say you are on a career campaign and are seeking information in their field. It is critical that you include in the letter that you don't expect them to have a job or to know of one available. You are only seeking information, and you will not take up more than 15 or 20 minutes of their time. Tell them that you will call them—give them a specific day—to set up an appointment.

"Here, Beth, is where your organizational skills are very important because you will be making a lot of contacts, and it will be important for you to keep a calendar of when you are supposed to call people and when your appointments are. First impressions are critical. If you tell a decision maker you will call him on Wednesday and you don't call until Friday, you may never overcome the negative impression that this would make. By the way, if you call on Wednesday and the decision maker isn't in, do not leave your name and number for him/her to call back. A good sales person always wants to keep control. You can leave your name and tell the secretary you will also be in and out and will try back later. Is there a time she would suggest? If the secretary is reluctant to put the call through, tell her the decision maker is expecting your call. Always be very courteous to secretaries. As you know, they have much more power and influence than many people give them credit for, but don't discuss your business with them. They are there to protect their bosses, and they are likely to transfer your call to the personnel office."

* * *

". . . there are many fellow human/beings who are willing to help you, and they will be very flattered that you came to them for information."

* * *

"By the way, Jessica, since you bring up personnel, why don't I just go to them. Don't they know when a department is expanding or when someone is being promoted?"

"Good question, and the answer is sometimes they do and sometimes they don't. Either way, you are giving up your control to someone else, the personnel person, who, by the way, does not have final hiring power. All too often these people see themselves as a negative force rather than a positive force. In other words, they see themselves screening people out rather than bringing good people in. They also must play by the rules. If they have a job order for a Public Relations Assistant with a college degree, they will knock you out of the running immediately, whereas a decision maker can hire the person he/she thinks will do the best job without being confined by arbitrary rules. Also, personnel departments are like the Sunday ads, everybody goes there."

"Everything you have told me certainly makes sense, Jessica, but I guess I just don't understand why a decision maker would take the time to see me."

"Beth, some of the nicest, kindest, most concerned people I know are decision makers. In a society that spends so much time dwelling on the negative, it is a wonderfully positive comment that there are many fellow human beings who are very willing to help you, and they will be very flattered that you came to them for information.

"The last part of the approach to the decision maker is the

call to set up the appointment. Sandy said he was running about a half hour late, so I think we can take a few more minutes to go over it.

"This call is much the same as the call I make to set up an appointment to make a sales presentation to a prospect. The biggest objection I get to setting an appointment is, 'We don't need any software.' In the same vein, the biggest objection you will probably face in getting an appointment is, 'We don't have any openings.' You will need to persist in your answer that you don't expect them to have a job or know of one available, you are just seeking advice and information. Follow that statement up quickly with two appointment time alternatives by saying for example, 'Could we meet for fifteen or twenty minutes Wednesday morning or would Thursday afternoon be better?' Beth, since you have been in management, it is possible that someone could have called you for an informational interview. Let's role-play a phone call with you as the decision maker and me as the person wanting the informational interview. You give me some of the objections to the appointment that you think you might get when you call. Okay?"

"Okay, I'd like to hear your answers to some of my objections!"

"Good. Let's start. Ring...Ring..."

"Hello. This is Beth Hoelster. May I help you?"

"Hi. This is Jessica Turney. I'm calling to follow up on the letter that I sent you. Did you receive it?"

"Yes, Jessica, I did."

"Great! As I mentioned in the letter, I don't expect you to have a position available or know of one. I'm requesting a brief meeting for some advice and information. Could we meet on Tuesday morning or would Thursday afternoon be better?"

"Jessica, I'm really busy this time of year, and it would be difficult for me to schedule a meeting."

"I understand that you are busy. That is why I am asking for a brief meeting. I will keep it to fifteen or twenty minutes. It is important to me. Can we meet on Tuesday about 8:00 a.m. or would Thursday at 4:15 be better?"

"How about if we just talk over the phone?"

"Beth, I appreciate the offer, but one of my objectives is to get your opinion of the way I present myself, and I would like to meet with you in person. Can we meet on Wednesday morning or would Thursday afternoon be better?"

"Jessica, I want you to know that we do not have any openings at this time. What if I send your resume to personnel?"

"Thank you for offering to do that (or thank you for doing that if they already sent it), I'm afraid I didn't make myself clear. I'm not applying for a job. I'm asking for a brief meeting for advice and information. Can we meet on Tuesday morning or would Thursday afternoon be better?"

"Well, I don't know what I can tell you, but if you want to come in on Wednesday morning at 9:00, I can give you a few minutes."

"Thank you very much, Beth. I appreciate it. I will see you on Wednesday morning at 9:00. Thanks again."

"Boy, Jessica! That could sound really pushy, couldn't it?"

"Yes, I guess it could. But it could also show some good qualities like being strongly career minded, enthusiastic, and assertive which could be important assets in many positions. So don't just think of it as negative. Your goal is to get in front of as many decision makers as possible. Remember, in sales, numbers are important. To make one sale, you have to make your presentation to many prospective clients (the number varies with the product), and to get a job you have to present yourself to many prospective employers. It is the rare individual who goes out on one interview and gets the job!"

"Jessica, I had one more question. What if I call the decision maker and they say they did not get the letter?"

"Then just give them a brief overview of the letter and ask for the appointment. Beth, I know we can not cover every objection you might get. I think you asked me the most common ones. Just remember, whatever their objection, try to overcome it and ask for the appointment.

"Come on! We'd better get over to Sandy's!"

Before you continue . . .

Get the latest edition of your city's Sunday paper and pull out the employment section. With a pen in hand, read the employment ads from A to Z. Circle all the ads that sound interesting to you either because of the job description or the industry. Remember, you are not necessarily looking for a job at this point; you are just identifying career fields and industries that you think you would enjoy.

It would also be valuable to pretend you are on the phone setting up an appointment for an informational interview. What would you say?

This should be a fun assignment! When you are done, you will have finished the third secret step.

Chapter Six

SECRET STEP 4— THE THEORY BEHIND THE INFORMATIONAL AND JOB INTERVIEW

We walked up the tree shaded sidewalk to Sandy's apartment. I was feeling a little nervous about meeting him and having to talk about my failures with this stranger.

"This is the one," Jessica said as we walked up the stairs to Sandy's apartment.

Jessica knocked on the door and it was opened by a middle aged man in a knit red shirt, khaki shorts, and tennis shoes. He had light brown hair that had started to recede.

"Hi, Jessica! And you must be Beth," he said as he smiled a broad, warm smile and shook my hand. "Please, ladies, come in."

Sandy's apartment was laid out like Jessica's, but instead of the modern pastel look, Sandy's apartment had a more lived in look. There was a big, cocoa brown corduroy couch with overstuffed pillows and matching love seat surrounding a round walnut coffee table. Sandy also had a big screen T.V. flanked by a stereo system. In the dining L, he had a walnut dining room set. The furnishing gave off a warmth just like Sandy did, and I knew I could relax and feel comfortable. I heard the music of 'Chicago' in the background.

"Beth, you must be tired and hungry. From what Jessica told me when she last called, she has been working you pretty hard. Come and have a seat on the deck."

Sandy's deck, like Jessica's, overlooked a natural, heavily wooded setting. Some of the tree branches actually hung over the deck, and Sandy had strung a couple bird feeders from them.

"I love your apartment, Sandy." I said, as I sat down on a large redwood chair. "This deck is fabulous. Do you get many birds?"

"Yes, I do. Mainly, the common ones like bluejays, cardinals and sparrows. But, no matter how common, they bring me a lot of enjoyment.

"I bet you and Jessica are starving. How about if we start eating. I have some boiled shrimp, sesame wafers, and fresh lemonade." Sandy disappeared into the apartment and returned with his tray filled with food and drink. He put the appetizers on the redwood table that was sitting in the middle of four large chairs. "Help yourselves," he said, as he poured the lemonade.

"Sandy, this is wonderful shrimp," Jessica said.

"It sure is, Sandy," I echoed. "Sandy, I want to thank you for all your help. I know we just met, but Jessica has given me so many lists and forms she said you created, that I feel you have been one of my advisors from the beginning. Everything you developed has been so helpful, especially that resume outline. It made writing the resume so much easier. I guess because I felt like all I had to do was fill in the blanks."

"I'm really glad everything was so helpful to you, Beth. My goal is to make this very stressful and frustrating time in a person's life a little easier, and I appreciate your comments. I'm very proud of the resume outline. Now, before you ladies get totally full, let's move over to the picnic table and eat dinner. I have barbecue pork steaks, roasted potatoes, and three layer salad."

As we sat eating what seemed to me to be one of the

most wonderful dinners I had ever had, Jessica chatted away about everything we had done throughout the day, relating to Sandy conversations we had and asking his opinion about the various situations. It was delightful to watch the two of them conferring like two doctors on a case. They obviously loved talking about career problems, and I was enjoying the opportunity to relax and not think.

"Sandy, that was a fabulous dinner," I said, as we all were finishing. "I want the recipe for everything!"

"Sandy is a gourmet cook," Jessica said proudly, "and I am going to weigh a ton!"

"Flattery will get you everywhere, ladies. Let me take these dishes in and bring out dessert." Sandy took the tray, loaded it up with dirty dishes, and disappeared into the apartment. When he came back, the tray had a new burden of chocolate torte cake and coffee. Jessica started serving the cake and coffee and Sandy said, "Jessica tells me you are at the point where you have set the appointment and now you are ready for the actual interview."

"That's right," I said.

"May I look at your resume, please?"

"Sure," I said, as I pulled it out of my notebook.

Sandy looked over the resume for several minutes while

Jessica and I waited to hear his opinion.

"This looks very good," Sandy finally said. "You know, Beth, you have covered a tremendous amount of material in a very short time. Don't feel you should have absorbed everything you and Jessica talked about, that wouldn't be possible. But, if you go over your notes and all the examples Jessica gave you several times, I think you will get all the important basics you will need to know to be successful. Now, if you are ready to start again, I would like to explain the theories of the two types of interviews: the informational interview and the job interview."

"I'm ready!" I said as I picked up my notebook and pen.

"Let's start with the informational interview. As you know from Jessica, all of this is built on a sales philosophy. Given that, if you had a new product that you were really excited about marketing, but it was rather unique and you really weren't sure who would use it, what do you think you would do?"

"Jessica already gave me a big hint to the answer on this one. I would go see decision makers in companies I thought could use my product."

"You learn fast, Beth. What do you think you would do once you got appointments set up with these decision makers and you were actually in one of their offices?"

"I think I would have to ask the decision maker a lot of questions."

"That's exactly right. Why do you think you would have to ask them a lot of questions?"

"How else could I find out if they would be right for my product and visa versa?"

"Correct again," Sandy said as he smiled his warm smile. "What kind of questions do you think you would ask?"

I hesitated a moment to think about it and then said, "I think I would ask what the needs of the company were, how big they were, what they saw as their future needs, did they have a product like mine, did they think their company would use a product like mine, and, since you said it was a new product, Sandy, I think I would ask them what they thought of my product and if they knew anyone else who could use it."

"Beth, believe it or not, you have described the informational interview. Just substitute yourself for the product. Let me give you a little bit more of the philosophy behind this kind of meeting.

"First of all, when you call a meeting, whether it's in your department, your company, or someone else's company, since you called it you set the agenda. So when you go on an informational interview, sit down before the meeting and think about what points you want to cover and what important information about yourself you want to be sure and mention. I highly suggest you write this out before you go. As with any first time meeting with someone you want to impress, you need to start out by establishing a good rapport. That includes meeting them with a firm handshake, a warm smile and good eye contact. You can have all the skills in the world, but if the decision maker doesn't like you, you won't be hired! Introducing very brief small talk or mentioning the contact person you both know should start you on a positive road. I also instruct my clients to use the decision maker's first name starting with the initial contact. This puts you on more of an equal footing and also gives you a little more control. It may not be proper etiquette, but it is very effective and rarely is anyone offended.

"Next, state your purpose. Why did you call this meeting? What is it you want to achieve? Outline the agenda you developed for the meeting. At this point it is polite and will make your meeting stronger, if you ask if this agenda is okay and get the DM's agreement. By the way, Beth, from now on I will refer to the decision maker as the DM and use the traditional male gender. Please be assured that does not mean that I believe all DM's are male, it just makes explaining so much material a little simpler if I am not always naming both genders.

"Now, you have set the stage to begin asking your questions. It is okay to refer to the questions. Have them neatly written on a pad and carry it in a nice binder. Remember, you only want to take 15 or 20 minutes of the DM's time, so choose your questions carefully and don't get lost in a lot of chit chat. Keep control! Basically, your list of questions was right on target, but I think it will help you if I can give you even more specific questions and the reasons behind them.

"After building rapport, you can start your questions by asking the DM how long he has been in the industry, how he got started, how he sees career development in the industry, and what frustrations he may have in that industry (or career field). As the DM responds to these questions, you will want to listen well, and where it's appropriate, make a comment that shows an accomplishment and/or skill that would be useful to the DM in the situation that he just described. For example, the DM might say he is frustrated because too many customer complaints that should be handled on a lower level are ending up on his desk. You can answer that you know that can be frustrating. The manager in your last job had the same problem before you came, and you were able to assess where the problem was and implement solutions resulting in the lowest level of customer complaints in five years. Beth, if during the course of the conversation you can insert some of your top skills and achievements, you plant the seed in the DM's mind that maybe there might be a place for you in his organization. Like the achievement I just mentioned, you can use the same skills and achievements that are on your resume.

"After you have asked industry questions, you can move to more specific job questions: what is the range of salary one can expect in that job; how does the DM see your background fitting into that kind of job; how does the DM see you coming across in an interview; does he have any suggestions? Does he see your objective as realistic?"

"Really? I can ask him salary questions or personal questions about myself? I thought that was forbidden on a job interview."

"You are right, Beth. You wouldn't want to ask salary questions or questions about your personal performance on a job interview. But this isn't a job interview, it's an informational interview, and the information you are asking for is important for you to know. That's the beauty of the informational interview. You are allowed to ask a lot of questions that would not be appropriate for you to ask on a job interview.

"As you end, be enthusiastic. Tell the DM how much you appreciate his time. Ask him how he would suggest you proceed from there? Whom else would he suggest for you to talk with to better understand the industry or advise you on career objectives. As in all sales, referrals are important so don't be afraid to ask. As you leave, thank the DM again for his time. Ask if you can keep him informed of your progress. This gives you an opportunity to keep up active contact with the DM. When you get home write the DM a thank you letter immediately. This can be brief. You would want to thank the DM for all his valuable advice and tell him how excited you are about working in his field. Try to mention something specific the DM said in the meeting to show you were a good listener. End by telling the DM you will keep him posted on your progress.

"Beware, Beth, sometimes in an informational interview, you will realize that you are actually in a job interview. In other words, although you didn't know it, there is a position available and the DM is interviewing you for it. This often happens when an individual is on an informational interview and is one very good reason to go on several! If you think that it is happening proceed as though you are on a job interview, not an informational interview. In other words, you wouldn't ask some of those questions we were talking about, and you would want to answer the DM's questions in the way you will learn to answer job interview questions. Another situation that might arise in an informational interview is a DM who is really enjoying talking to you and you see the time is going over the 20 minutes you had set as the meeting length. You would want to stop the interview by making a comment such as, 'I see my twenty minutes are up, and I want to keep my word and not take up any more of your time.' The DM will probably tell you that it's fine and not to worry about it. Then you can proceed as long as he wants to continue to talk.

"Does this all make sense to you, Beth?"

"Yes, but I am concerned if I will really know how to respond to the DM's remarks."

"The key is to know your skills and achievements very well. This is one reason I think it is essential that people write their own resumes and not have a service do it. When you are in an informational interview, you cannot always anticipate what the other person will say. But if you know yourself well, you can plug in positive comments that are appropriate to the conversation. The informational interview as well as the job interview require practice. The more interviews you can go on, the better you will get.

"Let's move on to the job interview. In the job interview, the employer is calling you for the interview so it's his meeting and his agenda. You approach the initial introduction in the same manner as the informational interview: smile, hand shake, lots of enthusiasm. On a job interview, you want to establish your ability to help the DM reach his goals. You accomplish this by answering questions in a positive manner, focusing on your strengths, not on your limitations, and trying to relate a few of your top achievements. Never—I repeat, Beth—never discuss a weakness or an insecurity. One of the most often asked questions in the interview is 'What is your weakest point?' It is your task to take a negative and make it a positive. Like, 'my weakest point is that sometimes I am too hard on myself because I demand excellence in all I do.' If the DM touches a weak point such as, 'I am concerned that you don't have any experience in this area' try to turn the objection around by saying something such as, 'While I have not worked in this industry specifically, the skills you are looking for, organization and good communication skills, are my strengths. For example, I reorganized an

107

* * *

*". . . never discuss a
weakness or an
insecurity."*

* * *

entire office and had them processing more business than they ever had. While people can learn a new industry, they may never be able to develop good organizational skills. Don't you think proven skills would be more valuable to you than industry experience?'

"If salary questions come up, do not give your salary requirement. If you mention a figure that is too high, it may disqualify you, and if you mention a figure that is too low, it will hurt your negotiations. You also don't want to give your previous salaries. What you are paid for the new job should be based on that job description not on your previous job."

"I agree, Sandy, that would be ideal, but I've been on interviews before, and they almost always ask either what you made previously or what you expect to make. How can you avoid answering the question without creating tension?"

"Maybe there will be a little tension, but I still believe it best for you not to talk about salary until the job is offered. If you refuse nicely, it will not cost you the job. In fact, you may even gain some respect. I have developed four answers that can be used for the salary question. Most of the time, these will work and the interviewer will move on to another question. I suggest you memorize these answers because this is the question that may cause you the most stress, and it will be easier for you if you can repeat the answer without having to think too much. I suggest you write this down." As Sandy talked I wrote on my pad:

1. How much are you currently making? Answer: "It is commensurate with the duties and responsibilities of the position."

2. What salary would you require? Answer: "I feel it should be based on the duties and responsibilities of the position. For the right position, I am willing to be flexible."

3. I need to know what range you would require. Answer: "I'm certain that you are prepared to make a fair offer and I would imagine you have a range in mind. What is your range for the position?" Whatever range they tell you, you would answer, "I feel comfortable that we can work out the salary."

4. If they still push you and won't give up. Answer: "I prefer not to talk about compensation until a position has been offered. Are you offering me the position?"

"Beth, most people won't push you that hard. But you need to be prepared with these answers."

"I hope I can do it, Sandy. I have to tell you, it makes me a little tense."

"I understand your feelings, Beth. But how tense do you think you would feel if you answered the salary question and then found out that you could have gotten a starting salary one, two, or even five thousand dollars higher than the figure you stated?"

"I see your point."

"I thought you would. By the way, you can use the same answer, commensurate with duties, when filling out an application.

"As with the informational interview, you will want to write a nice thank you letter when you get home. In the letter you can reaffirm the skills and qualities that will make you effective in the position. Also, if there is an important point that you forgot to make in the interview, you can mention it in the thank you letter. I will give you an example of a thank you letter for both the informational and job interview before you leave tonight.

"Beth, there is one last area we need to touch on that I know is very sensitive, and that is what you should say if they ask what happened in your previous position. Jessica filled me in on what happened earlier today which gave me a chance to think about an answer. What I suggest you say is something to the effect that as an experiment the home office hired you as the office manager under the branch manager and that you were hired to implement new policies and procedures. You did this very successfully, allowing the office to double the flow of work they could handle. But, after a year, the home office decided they had to cut back on some of their management, and you were let go. Keep it short, and don't say anything negative about the company or anyone in it. To paraphrase the Golden Rule, if you can't say anything positive, don't say anything at all."

"But is that really an honest answer, Sandy? Don't I need to explain what happened?"

"Beth, if you start explaining what happened, you will sound defensive. If you tell a future employer that the people at your last job didn't like you, it will scare him off even if the problem really had nothing to do with you personally. People who get fired are in a no win situation when it comes to explaining it to the next employer. So my advice is to try and find some non-personal reason for your termination and follow it up with a positive achievement from that job. Above all, keep the whole answer down to two or three sentences!

"I know this may sound difficult now, Beth, but if you concentrate on turning everything into a positive, I promise, with experience it will get easier. But, it takes work. After every interview, when you go home try and analyze what happened, what you said, and how you might have made a stronger statement. Write it down and review it for the next interview. One other word of advice, go on as many inter-views as you can, both informational and job interviews. So often, I hear people prejudge an interview saying things like informational interviews are pointless. Again, just like sales, it's a mathematical formula. Sales people know that they have to give X number of presentations to make a sale. (The number varies with each product.) So it is in the job search. You will have to have X number of interviews to find the right job. I tell my clients to go on every interview they can. You never know where an interview will take you. Maybe the job you are interviewing for isn't the right job for you, but often the DM will say that they may have another position available soon that fits your profile. Besides, every interview gives you the opportunity to practice so that when you do get to the 'important' interview, the one for the job you really want, you will have really honed your interviewing skills.

"Beth, I think you have had enough information for one day. If it is okay with you, I would like you to go home and go over your notes and resume. Tomorrow, we will do some role playing on the informational and job interview and talk about negotiating salary. Then you will be ready to go out and get started!"

"Sandy, I can't thank you and Jessica enough for all your help. Just saying I really appreciate it doesn't begin to express my feelings."

"You're welcome, Beth. Actually, Jessica and I get a lot of pleasure from seeing our system at work. I'll go get those examples of thank you letters for you."

"We really do get a lot of pleasure from teaching the system," Jessica said as Sandy left the room to get the letters.

"Now, go home, do your homework, and be back at my apartment at 10:30."

Sandy handed me the letters, and I put them with all my notes. I said good night to him and Jessica and drove home. I knew I had to do some homework, but first I was going to look at those plans I had for the apartments. I rushed up to my apartment, threw my notebook on the table, and opened the envelope Ruth gave me with the information about the apartments. I felt like a child on Christmas opening up a big present that had been under the tree. I spread the plans over my bed and began examining them. They all look wonderful, I thought, and the prices aren't too bad, especially if I get a raise in my next position. I saw a lot of kids at the pool that are Andy's age. I think he will really like it there, and I know it's in a good school district. I felt a renewed excitement about starting a new job (hopefully) in a new apartment. Decorating ideas were going through my mind as I washed up and put on a comfortable robe, and then I sat down with all my notes to study. When I next looked up at the clock I saw that it was 1:30 a.m. Get some sleep, Beth, or you won't be very sharp tomorrow. I crawled into my bed, set the alarm for 8:00 a.m. and fell asleep just about the time my head hit the pillow.

Exhibit J

THANK YOU LETTER FOR AN
INFORMATIONAL INTERVIEW

November 6, 1992

John Smith
Director of Development
Applebee, Inc.
1111 Pear Street
Cardinal, MO 66666

Dear John:

    Thank you for meeting with me today and sharing information about the toy business and how my skills might be used within this challenging industry. It is refreshing to hear someone speak of their company with such excitement and enthusiasm! I think your innovative idea of rewarding your employees for new toy designs is a good one. I will be interested to know how that works out for you.

    I appreciate your comments on how I present myself and your ideas of what steps I might take now in my career search. I will keep you informed of my progress.

Most sincerely,

Martha Washington
8214 Heritage Street
Cardinal, MO 66656
(314)111-2121

Exhibit K

THANK YOU LETTER FOR JOB INTERVIEW

Robert Stevenson
President
Peachtree Corporation
1234 King Street
Suite 100
Cardinal, MO 66621

Dear Bob:

It was a pleasure meeting with you today and learning about the needs of your department. The computer conversion that you are planning sounds both exciting and challenging. As a computer programmer, I have been involved in two conversions. Each time I completed the projects under budget and ahead of schedule.

I am excited about bringing my experience to Peachtree, and I feel I could make a substantial contribution to your team. I look forward to meeting with you again to further discuss your opportunity and how my skills can benefit your firm.

Sincerely,

Martha Washington
8214 Heritage Street
Cardinal, MO 66656
(314)111-2121

Before you continue . . .

Make your list of people to approach for an informational interview. Set a goal for yourself to get at least 20 names to begin with. If you are really ambitious, start writing your approach letters, but wait until you finish the book to send them. We want to be sure you are ready to interview!

Chapter Seven

SECRET STEP 5—
INTERVIEW SAMPLE
AND "THE CLOSE"

I heard the alarm rudely go off in the middle of a wonderful dream I was having about hiking in the forest. I rolled over and turned the horrible buzz off. That dream must have come from sitting on Sandy's deck, I thought. The idea of having to role play with Jessica and Sandy pushed me to get up and shower and dress quickly so that I would have some time to study. Looking at my limited wardrobe, I decided to dress as though I really were going to interview. Let's see, dark suit, white shirt for men or, for women, a nice blouse that's not too flashy. Polished shoes, not much jewelry, no perfume or cologne, and light on the make-up. Funny how I have always remembered those rules from a magazine article I read years ago, and they have served me well.

I dressed and read my notes while I had coffee and cereal. I felt as excited and nervous as though I were going to an actual interview. It's time to go, I thought as I glanced at the clock.

It was another lovely summer morning. I enjoyed the drive to Jessica's apartment, arriving there just at 10:30. "Good morning, Jessica," I said as she opened the door.

"Beth, come in. You look great! Good for you, you decided to dress the part."

The doorbell rang and Sandy came in. Both Sandy and Jessica were in jeans and polo shirts, but I was happy that I had dressed as though I were actually going on an interview. It made me feel more confident and professional.

"Good morning, Jessica and Beth. It's a glorious day out! How are you doing, Beth? Did we totally wear you out?"

"No, I feel great and ready to go!"

"Let's go into my office," Jessica said. "It's set-up like a typical office you would interview in."

We went into Jessica's office. She had a large desk with a computer on it, white bookshelves to the side of the desk, and two comfortable looking chairs in front of the desk. "I often bring trainees here to role play when I am doing weekend training." Jessica said. "Sandy, what do you think we should do first?"

"I think we should do the informational interview first, Jessica, with me interviewing you and you playing the part of Beth. You know Beth better than I do, and I think you would do a better job of answering questions for her than I would. Beth, I am having Jessica do this role play for you to watch because I think you will get more out of it than if you do it. As we discussed, informational interviews are very different from job interviews and I want you to see how to handle it.

"After we do the informational interview, I would like you and Jessica to do a job interview. Is that okay with you?"

"That's fine with me, Sandy," I said rather relieved.

"Are you ready to go, Jessica?"

Jessica sat down in the chair facing the desk and said "I'm ready."

Sandy got behind the desk, and I sat next to Jessica with my pen and notebook in hand. "Let's start, then," he said. "What field do you think Beth would like to get more information about?"

"Beth thinks that she might like the area of special events planning. So, why don't we do an informational interview about that. We can pretend that I referred her."

"That sounds fine. Let's start from the very beginning where Beth actually comes into the office."

Jessica got up, went outside her office door and knocked on the open door. Sandy got up from his chair and said, "You must be Beth Holester."

Jessica stretched her hand out, smiled and said, "Yes, I am. I am very pleased to meet you. Jessica has spoken very highly of you. I'm glad I have this opportunity to talk with you in person."

"Beth, please have a seat."

"Sandy, I'd like to thank you for meeting with me today. As I mentioned in my letter, I am on a career search. I don't expect you to have a position available or know of one. What would be of help to me is some advice and information. I have identified some strengths that I have that I would like to use in my next position, and some of those are developing and executing plans, creating ideas, and communicating with the public. I have identified special events planning as a career field where I feel I would have an interest and I would also be able to use my strengths. Your name was referred to me as someone who is an expert in special events planning, and what I'd like to do is ask you some questions about the field and how I might fit into it. Would that be alright?"

"Sure, that would be fine."

"Sandy, as I get around and speak to people, I find it fascinating to hear how people's career's have developed, and I would be interested to know how your career has developed."

"I started in the company about five years ago as a sales person, then I was promoted to regional sales manager. As the company grew, I was also put in charge of special events planning. In today's corporate world, we are all expected to wear many hats."

"I know what you mean about wearing many hats. In my last position I was in charge of seminar planning as well as all the office administrative duties, but I really found it challenging and I enjoyed the variety. Could you tell me a little about the duties of a Meeting Planner?"

"It covers everything big and small from regional meetings of our staff to two day training sessions. We also have monthly training luncheons for clients. These luncheons rotate around different locations in our region. I guess I would say the most important thing one has to do in this job besides keeping everything organized and on schedule is to handle all the clients' questions and problems."

"I understand what a challenge that can be! I also had the

responsibility of assessing customer's problems and implementing solutions. I enjoy that challenge and feel good about the fact that while working in this area, we had the lowest level of customer complaints in five years.

"Sandy, what kind of demand is there for Events Planners?"

"To tell you the truth, Beth, I am not sure. In my company, I have been doing it, but I think the time is quickly coming where I will need a support person to help me with it. It just takes up too much of my time that I think could be spent in a more productive manner."

"How do you feel someone with my background fits into this field?"

"Well, from what you have said, and from your resume, I would say you are very strong on the organizational end but a little weak on experience."

"I appreciate your critique. It's very helpful to me. I'm hoping that the experience that I've had in fund-raising events as well as coordinating seminars at my company will transfer to this field. What do you think?"

"Yes, I think it will be of benefit."

"If I were to enter the meeting and planning field, what kind of compensation do you think I could expect?"

"I would think from the low to mid-twenty's."

"Do you have any suggestions about the way I present myself?"

"No, Beth. I think you come across as very energetic and enthusiastic."

"Thank you, Sandy. I appreciate your meeting with me today. The information that you have shared is very helpful. Who else would you suggest I talk with?"

"I know a women at Lincoln College who does meeting and planning for parents and alumni. She is very nice, and I think you would enjoy talking with her. I have her name on my Rolodex. It's Carrie Long, 555-9315."

"Thank you again, Sandy. You have been very helpful. Would you mind if I keep you informed of my progress?"

"No, not at all, I would like to know how things turn out for you. If there is anything else I can do, please call."

Jessica stood up, shook Sandy's hand, and walked out of the office.

"That was great, you guys. Is that all there is to it?"

"That's it, Beth. But beware, not all decision makers will be as nice as Sandy or as helpful. If you meet one that isn't very helpful or is reluctant to talk, don't let it stop you, just go on to the next one. Do you have any questions?"

"Not that I can think of right now."

"Well then," Sandy said, "how about a five minute break and then we can do a job interview."

After we took a little break, we came back into Jessica's office. Jessica sat behind her desk, Sandy sat to the side, and I was sitting in front of Jessica. "Before we start, Beth, I think we had better decide what kind of job you are interviewing for. How about an Events Planner in a nation-wide insurance company?" Jessica said.

"Sounds fine to me. Let's start." I got up and walked outside of Jessica's office like she had done for the informational interview and knocked on the door.

"Good morning, Beth. I have been expecting you."

"Good morning, Jessica," I said shaking her hand.

"Please come in and have a seat."

"Thank you. I've been excited about interviewing with your company since I read the very nice article in last week's business journal. I bet you were pleased with it."

"Yes, we were. Thank you for mentioning it. Beth, if you

wouldn't mind, I'd like to get right into the interview and ask you some questions. Would you tell me something about yourself?"

"I'd be happy to. I'm hard working, well organized, and conscientious, and I'm good at developing and executing plans, creating ideas, and communicating with the public."

"Why are you interested in this position?"

"I've identified special events planning as the career field I would like to pursue because it uses the skills that I have, such as making decisions, solving problems, and developing and implementing programs."

"If you have some weakness in regard to this position, what would it be?"

"There are always areas in which one could improve, and I make it a point to continue to develop my job skills by reading, taking classes, going to seminars and taking advantage of any other learning opportunity."

"You mentioned you were good at solving problems, could you give me an example?"

"In my last position, one of my responsibilities was dealing with customer problems. I developed, proposed, and implemented solutions which resulted in the lowest level of customer complaints in five years."

"Beth, why did you leave your last position?"

"I was hired by the home office to work as the office manager under the branch manager. I was asked to implement new policies and procedures. I did this very successfully, and the office doubled the flow of work they could handle. But, after a year, the home office decided they had to cut back on some of their management staff, and I was let go."

"I see. Have you had any experience coordinating events?"

"I created, organized and executed plans for a fund-raising event which resulted in the highest level of contributions in the organization's history. I also organized monthly seminars for my last company."

"What kind of salary would you require?"

"What I'm most interested in is a position where I can use the skills I've worked so hard to develop, doing work I really enjoy. For the right opportunity, I'm prepared to be flexible."

"Beth, I'm impressed with some of the things you've done, but I'm not sure you have the right qualifications for this position."

"What do you consider to be the best qualifications for this position?"

"Someone who has had at least one or two years of events planning experience."

"Jessica, I can understand your concern. Although I did not have the title of Events Planner, one of my responsibilities was to organize all of our monthly seminars. I am proud to say that all the seminar participants consistently rated the meetings as well organized, on schedule, and meaningful. Does that help with your concern?"

"Yes, Beth, it does. Do you have any questions about the position?"

"How would you describe the weekly activities of this person?"

"You are always looking about eight weeks ahead of any one event. Getting your mailing list together, developing and sending letters of invitation, reserving facilities and arranging for catering, rooms, or whatever is necessary. At the same time, you are checking on any current events taking place. Organizing the R.S.V.P. lists, talking to whomever is conducting the event to see what materials they may need prepared for the seminar and what kind of equipment they want set up for the seminar, such as a slide projector, podium, etc. You would also be responding to any events that may have just been held. Sending out thank you notes to client participants, compiling information from the evaluations we have them complete at the end of seminars, and so forth. So at any given time, you are dealing with the past, present and future, and you need to be able to keep all of it straight. How does that sound to you?"

"It sounds just like the kind of challenge and variety I enjoy! I'm really excited about the position, Jessica. What is the next step?"

"Well, I have a few more people I need to interview and then I will take what I consider to be the top five candidates and have the Executive Director of the Midwest region talk to them. I hope he will be able to interview people next week, and then he and I will make the final decision."

"Can I go ahead and schedule an interview time with him now while I am here?"

"No, I am not sure of his calendar, but I will have his secretary call the finalists and make the appointments."

"Jessica, I am glad I had the opportunity to talk with you, and I am looking forward to the opportunity to talk with the regional director."

"Good, Beth. We will keep in touch."

"Thank you." I got up and shook Jessica's hand as I would at the end of an interview.

"Beth, you did a great job!" Sandy said. "I really like how you asked for the next appointment. It showed real interest and assertiveness which would be an important quality for this job."

"Thank you, Sandy. I got so caught up in the role play, that I really was excited about the job and wanted to ask for the next interview. I'm glad that was okay."

"What you did, Beth," Jessica said, "is the final step of a sale. It is called the close. In this case you were trying to get him to set an appointment date or 'close' him on an appointment. The ultimate close in the job search is to ask for the job, negotiate the salary, and accept or reject the final offer. Sandy and I will go through the closing step with you. But, before we start that, Sandy, do you have any more information you would like to add about interviewing?"

"Beth, most jobs will require two or three interviews. Basically, they will be the same as we have discussed but with different people. Again, it's important to develop rapport with each person and establish your ability to help meet the needs of that person. End every interview by asking what the next step is."

Jessica looked at the clock on her desk and said, "Before we start on the close, why don't we order some pizza and take a break."

"Sounds good to me," I said.

"Me too!" said Sandy.

We all stood up and went into Jessica's living room. "How about one pepperoni and one mushroom," she asked.

"Sounds perfect," answered Sandy. "Okay with you, Beth?"

"Mushroom is my favorite!"

"I know you two," Jessica laughed, as she picked up the phone to order the pizza.

"Beth, you are about done with training. How do you feel?" Sandy said.

"I feel great! I have learned so much from the two of you. I want to implement what you have taught me to the best of my ability to show you how much I appreciate the time and effort you have put into my training."

"You just get yourself a job that you will enjoy and we will be happy," Jessica said.

When the pizza came, we went out on the deck to eat and listen to the birds.

"That was a nice break," Jessica said. "But we better get back to work if we are going to finish by dinner time."

"I'll second that. I'm supposed to pick up Andy by 5:00 p.m."

"Let's go into the living room and get started, then," Jessica said.

We got settled and Jessica said, "At some point, you want to try and get the offer. Usually this will happen at the end of the second or third interview or when you feel you have answered all the questions they have and there is no one else you are supposed to interview with. At that point you can say something such as, 'What questions can I answer before you would offer me the position?' or you can use this close immediately after you have made a strong statement about yourself such as, 'I feel confident that with my organizational skills and my ability to communicate effectively both in writing and orally, I will be able to make a significant contribution to your department. Are there any other questions you would like me to answer before you would offer me the position?' Remember, in sales, you may have to close more than once. In other words, they may ask you another question. You would answer it, and use your close again using the same words. Sometimes people have a hard time making the final decision; they are afraid they may make a mistake. By closing, you are helping the decision maker make the decision (to hire you, hopefully)."

"Won't they just think I'm pushy?"

"No, I don't think so. You are not asking in a way that would be obnoxious. What you are really saying is that you want the position and you feel you can do a good job. After all, if you are not confident about yourself and your abilities,

133

* * *

*"... you are not
going to get what
you are worth, you
are going to get
what you
negotiate."*

* * *

why should the decision maker be confident about you. I truly think that asking for the job is a positive action."

"Do you have any more questions about this close?"

"No, I understand what you want me to do. Knowing me, if I am excited about the position, it won't be hard to ask for the job."

"Good! Then I think the last thing you need to learn is how to negotiate your salary. Sandy, this is your favorite part of the process, so why don't you explain it."

"My pleasure. Beth, as we discussed earlier when we talked about the salary question, you don't want to talk salary or try to negotiate for something until the position is offered. Once they have offered you the position, they have said that they want you which puts you in a place of strength. One rule I want you to remember is that you are not going to get what you are worth, you are going to get what you negotiate. ALWAYS TRY TO NEGOTIATE! In almost every situation, there is a range of dollars available, and the first number is almost always the lowest number in the range. Your goal is to negotiate an amount as high in the range as you can.

"The usual scenario is that they say they would like to hire you and that they are going to start you at x amount of dollars. This amount may be higher than what you had anticipated, but you still want to try and negotiate! Your first reaction is to use what I call thoughtful silence. You can look down and just appear as though you are giving it thought. This lets them know that you are considering the offer, but that it's unsatisfactory. This may feel tense, but it works most of the time. Let the other person talk first. Often, at this point, the person hiring you will increase the offer without you saying anything."

"What should I do if they don't say anything?"

"If they don't say anything or if you are too uncomfortable with this close, make the statement that you are excited about the opportunity and look forward to working with them. You feel you can make a significant contribution, but you feel the offer is on the low side. THEN BE QUIET!

"They will probably either offer a little more or tell you that is what is in their budget. Your next step is (briefly) to recap the responsibilities of the position by saying something to the effect that you think it's important that your compensation be based on the duties and responsibilities of the position and the contribution you can make. Then go over those points again by saying, you want me to—(list the responsibilities of the job), and then say that based on these responsibilities and your proven skills and abilities to carry these responsibilities out, you feel the salary is a little low. They may say, 'Well what do you need?' Your answer should be that you need their very best offer."

"Sandy, I'm getting nervous just hearing you talk about negotiating."

136

"Negotiating is hard, but if you don't try at least once to raise the salary, you have probably sold yourself too low."

"How will I know what kind of salary I should be shooting for?"

"Data you have gathered from your advice and information meetings should have given you an idea of what your worth is, and you want to try to get that amount."

"I have heard through the grapevine that many companies tell you the worth of the fringe benefits when they tell you salary amount. Should I count that in?"

"Definitely not! It is certainly okay to ask about fringe benefits if it's important to you, but don't let them make it part of the salary. Think about it; when is the last time you went into the grocery store and bought milk and bread with a term life insurance policy—you can't do it."

"Good point, Sandy."

"When you feel you have negotiated for as much as you can, ask for a review and salary increase in six months based on your merit. There is nothing unusual about a six month review, so don't be shy about it. Once you feel completely finished with salary, your review, and information about your benefits, ask the person hiring you to put the offer in writing so that you both know the salary, the fringe benefits, the review schedule, and the starting date. You may also want to ask for 24 hours to think it over. You may have some concerns you want to think about or there may be another opportunity you would really prefer. The twenty-four hours will give you a chance to call another employer where there is an opportunity pending and tell him them that his position is your first choice, but you have an offer pending. Ask him if he could expedite his decision? Not only will this push him a little, but it makes you look stronger. It will also give you some leverage in salary negotiations."

"My biggest problem should be that I have two offers to choose from!"

"Beth, you might be surprised. If you go after the job market aggressively and make it your full-time job, scheduling 10 or more interviews a week (and with informational interviewing, this is very realistic) you could quite possibly end up with two offers at once."

"I'm ready. First thing tomorrow, I will take my resume to the copy shop and start my research."

"Beth, you have been an excellent student. You have accepted the information with a good attitude. You would be surprised to hear how many of my clients argue with me and tell me the process won't work before they even try it. If you continue with this attitude, I see no reason why you should not be successful. It will take hard work and commitment on your part. Neither Jessica nor I would tell you otherwise. Most personal commitments take time and effort. Your commitment here is to the program we have taught you, and, most of all, to yourself: to find yourself the best position for your skills, and the best environment for your personality. Don't sell yourself short! You deserve success and happiness."

"Thank you, Jessica and Sandy. You both have been wonderful to give me your knowledge and your time. I will never forget you for this. After I am successful, I hope I will have an opportunity to help someone else the way you have helped me."

"Beth, call me if you have any questions."

"Thanks, Jessica. I better go get Andy and tell him what's going on. I am glad I waited. I really feel optimistic about our future. After I start my new job, I am going to make the two of you a fabulous dinner."

Before you continue . . .

Ask a friend to role play an informational interview (you may have to explain it to him/her first) and a job interview with you. If you can't find someone to role play with you, then become your favorite actor and play the role of the employer yourself! If you are on your own, speak out loud. Hearing your voice is important and will build confidence.

Practice! Practice! Practice!

Chapter Eight

SUCCESS!

"Welcome to the neighborhood," Jessica said as she handed me a beautiful bouquet of flowers.

"Thank you!" I said, bursting with pride as Jessica and Sandy came in.

"Beth, it looks wonderful! I love it!" Jessica said. "Take us on the grand tour. Why didn't you call us? We would have helped you move."

"You guys helped me so much already, I didn't want to ask you for more. Besides, I wanted to surprise you and have the apartment decorated when you came in. As you can see, my floor plan is different from yours. I have a little smaller living room/dining room combination than you and Sandy and a larger eat in kitchen. I wanted Andy to have a place where he and his friends could snack, and I wouldn't be worried about them spilling food on the carpet or ruining the dining room chairs."

"Your furniture looks new, Beth. I don't remember this gorgeous couch and love seat."

"For my birthday, my parents gave me a gift certificate to Prints & Chintz and I had my couch and love seat recovered." I looked fondly at the burgundy and green rose pattern on the cream colored background. The sight of it had such a soothing effect on me. "I already had the walnut dining room set. I just recovered the chairs in Burgundy to match the couch. I really enjoy the kitchen," I said as I led them into it. "As you can see, this floor plan has the sliding glass doors to the deck off the kitchen. I look forward to cooking dinner now. While I'm cooking, I open the sliding door and listen to the birds and the wind in the branches and watch the sun go down. It's my favorite time of day. I found this darling table and chairs at Uncle Sam's Furniture Outlet," I said pointing to my bleached wood table with a white inlaid tile top and wood chairs to match.

"Beth, you find the best deals in town. I admire your

ability to decorate within a budget and not spare quality. You can give me lessons in this area!" Jessica said as she admired the table.

"The bedrooms are very large and they have great closet space! But, probably the best part of this apartment complex is how happy Andy is here. He started his new school, and a lot of the kids in his class live in these apartments. With the clubhouse, pool, park area, and trails through the woods, the kids have plenty to do here."

"Beth, you are absolutely glowing. I am glad to see you so happy," Sandy said. "Tell me how your job search went."

"It went very well," I said, "and it's all thanks to you and Jessica and what you taught me."

"Not quite, Beth. First you had to have the skills to market, and, most importantly, you had to be willing to get out there and do the work of looking for a job," Sandy retorted.

"Well, I'll admit it was work, but it was all worth it."

I had put the ice bucket and a selection of soft drinks and wine on the pass through bar between the kitchen and the dining room. "You and Jessica help yourselves to whatever you would like to drink, and make yourselves comfortable in the living room while I get the hors d'oeuvres." I took the tray of hot hors d'oeuvres out of the oven. "Let's see, the dill dip and bread are out on the coffee table with the fresh vegetables, so that should be it."

When we all got settled around the glass octagonal coffee table, I told Sandy and Jessica the story of my job search.

"The Monday morning after we met, I went to the copy shop and had my resume done as you suggested and purchased the bond paper and envelopes to match. I sent my resume to all the ads I was interested in from the Sunday paper using the 'I' letter form. By the way, that worked well. I even got some positive comments on it from interviewers. Then I let my fingers do the walking. Ever since my training with Jessica when I found the ad in the Sunday paper for an Events Planner in a hospital, I felt excited about the possibility of making it my career field. So, I decided I should pursue it with some informational interviews. I opened the Yellow Pages to hospitals. I called hospitals within commuting distance and asked for their Well Clinic Department. I then asked the person who answered the phone if they would give me the name of the person in charge of the clinic and his/her mailing address. That part was easy. Everyone I talked to was willing to give me the information I needed. Then I typed letters to these people using the example you gave me of an approach letter. After dinner, Andy and I drove to the Post Office and mailed all my letters. Then we celebrated with a trip to Dairy Queen for hot fudge sundaes.

"I didn't think it would be a good idea to put all my eggs in one basket, so the next day I went through the same process with several banks and got the names of New Accounts department heads and sent them approach letters. Tuesday night I started calling people I knew, asking for referrals for informational interviews. Most everyone I called was helpful, and I was able to develop several more contacts for informational interviews. By Friday, I was ready to start making calls about the letters I mailed Monday. I kept everything straight by making my own calendar in a three ring notebook. I marked several pages with the day and date just like you would find in a regular calendar, but the notebook gave me a lot more room for notations than a calendar would have. I had plenty of room on each page to list my appointments for the day as well as that day's 'to do' list. I also divided the notebook into three sections; a calendar section, an address section, and a section for general notes.

"Before my first informational interview, I was a basket case, but by the fifth, I was perfectly calm. I found pretty much what you told me I would. Some people were wonderful and some were not. On one of my informational interviews at a hospital, the woman I was meeting with told me she thought her division would be creating a new position for an Assistant Community Events Planner, and she would get back to me when she heard more. I asked her what she thought the time frame would be, and she said probably two to three weeks. Remembering your advice to keep control, I made a notation in my notebook to call her two weeks from our meeting. I also wrote her a thank you and mentioned I would call her in a few weeks. To make what already has been a long story a little shorter, that turned out to be the job I got. I had to interview three times for that position before it was offered to me, and I started work exactly 10 weeks from the day I started my job search."

"Beth, I didn't tell Sandy what you told me about the job. I thought you would like to do it."

"Sandy, the job is perfect for me. I am sure you have received fliers in your mail from the local hospitals advertising seminars and classes to help people stay well like classes in nutrition, stress management, weight loss, exercise, etc. My job is to help with setting up those classes and seminars, which includes writing material for brochures, getting speakers, reserving rooms, accepting reservations, and even attending many of the seminars as a 'good will ambassador' from the hospital. By being at the events, I'm also available for comments and suggestions. I just love my work, and they seem equally as happy with me. The hospital offers tuition reimbursement, and I plan to return to school in an adult degree program that meets one night a week. I think there is a good future for me in the events planning field, and a degree will certainly help."

"Beth, I am really glad to hear how successful you have been. It is very rewarding to me personally. Tell me, how did your salary negotiations go?"

"That was probably the hardest part for me. I did what you suggested and memorized the answers. I also did a lot of practicing in the privacy of my bedroom before I got to the actual interview. In the end, I was able to bring the initial offer up a little and also have them agree in writing to give me a six month job and salary review."

"It sounds like you did very well," Sandy said.

"What would you expect? I had great teachers!" I said with a smile.

"We had better go eat dinner before it disintegrates." I had set the dining room table with the fine china and crystal left to me by my grandmother. I had very few occasions that warranted getting out grandma's legacy, but showing Jessica and Sandy how important they were to me was certainly one of those occasions. I lit the white tapered candles that I had put into the brightly polished 65 year old brass candle holders (also from Grandma). I could see by the flickering reflection in Jessica's and Sandy's eyes that the significance of my efforts was not lost.

* * *

Don't sell yourself short! You deserve success and happiness.

* * *

Before you leave . . .

You are now ready for secret steps 4 and 5. It's up to you to take all you have learned and apply it to the job market. Please remember that sales is a mathematical game. You may hear 'no' many times before you hear 'yes'. Don't give up! In fact sales trainers tell you to say, 'Thank you very much' after every no because that brings you one step closer to the yes.

After you accept a job, write all your contacts throughout your job search and thank them for helping you (even if they didn't), and inform them of what you are doing and where you will be located. You have spent a lot of time building a network that may be of great value to you later in your career, and this last step is important. Besides, it's the right thing to do.

As your final assignment, Bob and I would also like you to write to us. We would enjoy hearing about the outcome of your job search. Please include any comments about the book that you would like to make.

Our very best wishes for your success!

THE AUTHORS

Barbara Siegel is president of The Career Consulting Group, a career consulting and seminar firm in St. Louis, Missouri. She attended the University of Colorado, Boulder, and received a Certificate in Writing for the Professional from Washington University, St. Louis, Missouri. She has ten years experience in sales and sales training and has sold for two international career consulting firms. Along with giving seminars and consulting with clients, Barbara makes numerous appearances on national radio and TV talk programs. She is also involved with a federally funded satellite training program on job search techniques that is based on her book and seen nationwide.

Robert Siegel is vice-president of Client Services for the St. Louis office of Haldane Associates, an international career consulting/outplacement corporation. He received his Master's Degree in Counseling from the University of Missouri. Before joining Haldane, he coordinated training programs for Anheuser-Busch, Monsanto, and General Dynamics as a national consultant for the world's largest training corporation.

The Siegels make their home in St. Louis with their cats, Tipper and Ziggy, and their dog, Benji. They have four grown children, Susan, Mark, Richie, and Melissa.

INDEX

CAREER RESOURCES

Contact Impact Publications to receive a free copy of their latest comprehensive and annotated catalog of over 1,500 career resources (books, subscriptions, training programs, videos, audiocassettes, computer software).

The following career resources, many of which are mentioned in previous chapters, are available directly from Impact Publications. Complete the following form or list the titles, include postage (see formula at the end), enclose payment, and send your order to:

IMPACT PUBLICATIONS
9104-N Manassas Drive
Manassas Park, VA 22111
Tel. 703/361-7300
FAX 703/335-9486

Orders from individuals must be prepaid by check, moneyorder, Visa or MasterCard number. We accept telephone and FAX orders with a Visa or MasterCard number.

Qty.	TITLES	Price	TOTAL

JOB SEARCH STRATEGIES & TACTICS

Qty.	TITLES	Price	TOTAL
___	Change Your Job, Change Your Life!	$14.95	_____
___	Complete Job Search Handbook	$12.95	_____
___	Dynamite Tele-Search	$10.95	_____
___	Five Secrets to Finding a Job	$12.95	_____
___	Go Hire Yourself an Employer	$9.95	_____
___	Guerrilla Tactics in the New Job Market	$5.99	_____
___	How to Get Interviews From Classified Job Ads	$14.95	_____
___	Joyce Lain Kennedy's Career Book	$29.95	_____

___ Knock 'Em Dead	$19.95	_____
___ Professional's Job Finder	$18.95	_____
___ Right Place At the Right Time	$11.95	_____
___ Rites of Passage At $100,000+	$29.95	_____
___ Super Job Search	$22.95	_____
___ Who's Hiring Who	$9.95	_____
___ Work in the New Economy	$14.95	_____

BEST JOBS AND EMPLOYERS FOR THE 90s

___ 100 Best Jobs For the 1990s and Beyond	$19.95	_____
___ 101 Careers	$12.95	_____
___ American Almanac of Jobs and Salaries	$17.95	_____
___ America's 50 Fastest Growing Jobs	$9.95	_____
___ America's Fastest Growing Employers	$14.95	_____
___ Best Jobs For the 1990s and Into the 21st Century	$12.95	_____
___ Hoover's Handbook of American Business (annual)	$34.95	_____
___ Hoover's Handbook of World Business (annual)	$32.95	_____
___ Job Seeker's Guide To 1000 Top Employers	$22.95	_____
___ Jobs! What They Are, Where They Are, What They Pay	$13.95	_____
___ Jobs 1993/1994	$15.95	_____
___ Jobs Rated Almanac	$15.95	_____
___ New Emerging Careers	$14.95	_____
___ Top Professions	$10.95	_____
___ Where the Jobs Are	$15.95	_____

KEY DIRECTORIES

___ Career Training Sourcebook	$24.95	_____
___ Careers Encyclopedia	$39.95	_____
___ Dictionary of Occupational Titles	$39.95	_____
___ Directory of Executive Recruiters (annual)	$44.95	_____
___ Directory of Outplacement Firms	$74.95	_____
___ Directory of Special Programs For Minority Group Members	$31.95	_____
___ Encyclopedia of Careers and Vocational Guidance	$129.95	_____
___ Enhanced Guide For Occupational Exploration	$29.95	_____
___ Government Directory of Addresses and Telephone Numbers	$99.95	_____
___ Internships (annual)	$29.95	_____
___ Job Bank Guide To Employment Services (annual)	$149.95	_____
___ Job Hunter's Sourcebook	$59.95	_____
___ Moving and Relocation Directory	$149.00	_____
___ National Directory of Addresses & Telephone Numbers	$129.95	_____
___ National Job Bank (annual)	$249.95	_____
___ National Trade and Professional Associations	$79.95	_____
___ Minority Organizations	$49.95	_____
___ Occupational Outlook Handbook	$22.95	_____
___ Professional Careers Sourcebook	$79.95	_____

CITY AND STATE JOB FINDERS

___ Jobs in Washington, DC $11.95   _____

How To Get a Job In . . .

___ Atlanta	$15.95	_____
___ Boston	$15.95	_____
___ Chicago	$15.95	_____
___ Dallas/Fort Worth	$15.95	_____
___ Houston	$15.95	_____
___ New York	$15.95	_____
___ San Francisco	$15.95	_____
___ Seattle/Portland	$15.95	_____
___ Southern California	$15.95	_____
___ Washington, DC	$15.95	_____

Bob Adams' Job Banks to:

___ Atlanta	$15.95	_____
___ Boston	$15.95	_____
___ Chicago	$15.95	_____
___ Dallas/Fort Worth	$15.95	_____
___ Denver	$15.95	_____
___ Detroit	$15.95	_____
___ Florida	$15.95	_____
___ Houston	$15.95	_____
___ Los Angeles	$15.95	_____
___ Minneapolis	$15.95	_____
___ New York	$15.95	_____
___ Ohio	$15.95	_____
___ Philadelphia	$15.95	_____
___ Phoenix	$15.95	_____
___ San Francisco	$15.95	_____
___ Seattle	$15.95	_____
___ Washington, DC	$15.95	_____

ALTERNATIVE JOBS AND CAREERS

___ Adventure Careers	$9.95	_____
___ Advertising Career Directory	$17.95	_____
___ Book Publishing Career Directory	$17.95	_____
___ Business and Finance Career Directory	$17.95	_____
___ But What If I Don't Want To Go To College?	$10.95	_____
___ Career Opportunities in Advertising and Public Relations	$27.95	_____
___ Career Opportunities in Art	$27.95	_____
___ Career Opportunities in the Music Industry	$27.95	_____
___ Career Opportunities in the Sports Industry	$27.95	_____
___ Career Opportunities in TV, Cable, and Video	$27.95	_____

___ Career Opportunities in Theater and Performing Arts	$27.95	___
___ Career Opportunities in Writing	$27.95	___
___ Careers For Animal Lovers	$12.95	___
___ Careers For Bookworms	$12.95	___
___ Careers For Foreign Language Speakers	$12.95	___
___ Careers For Good Samaritans	$12.95	___
___ Careers For Gourmets	$12.95	___
___ Careers For Nature Lovers	$12.95	___
___ Careers For Numbers Crunchers	$12.95	___
___ Careers For Sports Nuts	$12.95	___
___ Careers For Travel Buffs	$12.95	___
___ Careers in Computers	$16.95	___
___ Careers in Education	$16.95	___
___ Careers in Health Care	$16.95	___
___ Careers in High Tech	$16.95	___
___ Careers in Law	$16.95	___
___ Careers in Medicine	$16.95	___
___ Careers in Mental Health	$10.95	___
___ Careers in the Outdoors	$12.95	___
___ Encyclopedia of Career Choices For the 1990s	$19.95	___
___ Environmental Career Guide	$14.95	___
___ Environmental Jobs For Scientists and Engineers	$14.95	___
___ Health Care Job Explosion	$14.95	___
___ Healthcare Career Directory	$17.95	___
___ Magazine Publishing Career Directory	$17.95	___
___ Marketing and Sales Career Directory	$17.95	___
___ Newspaper Publishing Career Directory	$17.95	___
___ Opportunities in Accounting	$13.95	___
___ Opportunities in Advertising	$13.95	___
___ Opportunities in Biological Sciences	$13.95	___
___ Opportunities in Chemistry	$13.95	___
___ Opportunities in Civil Engineering	$13.95	___
___ Opportunities in Computer Science	$13.95	___
___ Opportunities in Counseling & Development	$13.95	___
___ Opportunities in Dental Care	$13.95	___
___ Opportunities in Electronic & Electrical Engineering	$13.95	___
___ Opportunities in Environmental Careers	$13.95	___
___ Opportunities in Financial Career	$13.95	___
___ Opportunities in Fitness	$13.95	___
___ Opportunities in Gerontology	$13.95	___
___ Opportunities in Health & Medical Careers	$13.95	___
___ Opportunities in Journalism	$13.95	___
___ Opportunities in Law	$13.95	___
___ Opportunities in Medical Technology	$13.95	___
___ Opportunities in Microelectronics	$13.95	___
___ Opportunities in Nursing	$13.95	___
___ Opportunities in Paralegal Careers	$13.95	___
___ Opportunities in Pharmacy	$13.95	___
___ Opportunities in Psychology	$13.95	___
___ Opportunities in Teaching	$13.95	___

___ Opportunities in Telecommunications $13.95 ___
___ Opportunities in Television & Video $13.95 ___
___ Opportunities in Veterinary Medicine $13.95 ___
___ Outdoor Careers $14.95 ___
___ Public Relations Career Directory $17.95 ___
___ Radio and Television Career Directory $17.95 ___
___ Travel and Hospitality Career Directory $17.95 ___

INTERNATIONAL & OVERSEAS JOBS

___ Almanac of International Jobs and Careers $14.95 ___
___ Complete Guide To International Jobs & Careers $13.95 ___
___ Guide To Careers in World Affairs $14.95 ___
___ How To Get a Job in Europe $17.95 ___
___ How To Get a Job in the Pacific Rim $17.95 ___
___ Jobs For People Who Love Travel $12.95 ___
___ Teaching English Abroad $13.95 ___

PUBLIC-ORIENTED CAREERS

___ Almanac of American Government Jobs and Careers $14.95 ___
___ Complete Guide To Public Employment $19.95 ___
___ Find a Federal Job Fast! $9.95 ___
___ Government Job Finder $14.95 ___
___ Right SF-171 Writer $19.95 ___

COMPUTER SOFTWARE

___ JOBHUNT Quick and Easy Employer Contacts $49.95 ___
___ INSTANT Job Hunting Letters $39.95 ___
___ ResumeMaker $49.95 ___

VIDEOS

___ Find the Job You Want...and Get It! (4 videos) $229.95 ___
___ How To Present a Professional Image (2 videos) $149.95 ___
___ Insider's Guide To Competitive Interviewing $59.95 ___
___ Networking Your Way To Success $89.95 ___
___ Winning At Job Hunting in the 90s $89.95 ___

JOB LISTINGS & VACANCY ANNOUNCEMENTS

___ Federal Career Opportunities (6 biweekly issues) $38.00 ___
___ International Employment Gazette (6 biweekly issues) $35.00 ___

SKILLS, TESTING, & SELF-ASSESSMENT

___ Discover the Best Jobs For You! $11.95 ___

___ What Color Is Your Parachute? $14.95 ___
___ Where Do I Go From Here With My Life? $10.95 ___

RESUMES, LETTERS, & NETWORKING

___ Dynamite Cover Letters $9.95 ___
___ Dynamite Resumes $9.95 ___
___ Great Connections $11.95 ___
___ High Impact Resumes and Letters $12.95 ___
___ Job Search Letters That Get Results $12.95 ___
___ New Network Your Way To Job and Career Success $12.95 ___

DRESS, APPEARANCE, IMAGE

___ John Molloy's New Dress For Success $10.95 ___
___ Red Socks Don't Work! $14.95 ___
___ Women's Dress For Success $9.95 ___

INTERVIEWS & SALARY NEGOTIATIONS

___ Dynamite Answers To Interview Questions $9.95 ___
___ Dynamite Salary Negotiation $12.95 ___
___ Interview For Success $11.95 ___

MILITARY

___ From Army Green to Corporate Gray $13.95 ___
___ Beyond the Uniform $12.95 ___
___ Civilian Career Guide $12.95 ___
___ Does Your Resume Wear Combat Boots? $9.95 ___
___ Job Search: Marketing Your Military Experience $14.95 ___
___ Re-Entry $13.95 ___
___ Retiring From the Military $22.95 ___

WOMEN AND SPOUSES

___ New Relocating Spouse's Guide to Employment $14.95 ___
___ Resumes For Re-Entry: A Handbook For Women $10.95 ___
___ Smart Woman's Guide to Resumes and Job Hunting $9.95 ___
___ Women's Job Search Handbook $12.95 ___

MINORITIES AND DISABLED

___ Directory of Special Programs For
Minority Group Members $31.95 ___
___ Job Hunting For People With Disabilities $14.95 ___
___ Minority Organizations $49.95 ___
___ Work, Sister, Work $19.95 ___

COLLEGE STUDENTS

___ College Majors and Careers	$15.95	_____
___ Graduating To the 9-5 World	$11.95	_____
___ Liberal Arts Jobs	$10.95	_____

SUBTOTAL _____

Virginia residents add 4½% sales tax _____

POSTAGE/HANDLING ($3.00 for first
title and $1.00 for each additional book) __$3.00__

Number of additional titles x $1.00 ----------- _____

TOTAL ENCLOSED ---------------- _____

SHIP TO:

NAME _____

ADDRESS _____

_____

_____

[ ] I enclose check/moneyorder for $ _____ made
payable to IMPACT PUBLICATIONS.

[ ] Please charge $ _____ to my credit card:

Card # _____

Expiration date: _____ / _____

Signature _____

SEND YOUR ORDER TO:

IMPACT PUBLICATIONS
9104-N Manassas Drive
Manassas Park, VA 22111
Fax 703/335-9486 (Visa/MasterCard)